MW01147728

The Message is a contemporary
rendering of the Bible from the original
languages, crafted to present its tone,
rhythm, events, and ideas
in everyday language.

+ + +

*The Message Student Devotional Bible:
Psalms* is excerpted from *The Message
Student Devotional Bible*. The full Bible
will be available from NavPress
in spring 2026.

A NavPress resource published in alliance
with Tyndale House Publishers

THE **MESSAGE**

STUDENT

PSALMS

BIBLE

DEVOTIONAL

E U G E N E   H .   P E T E R S O N

NavPress.com

The Message Student Devotional Bible: Psalms copyright © 2025 by The Navigators.

A NavPress resource published in alliance with Tyndale House Publishers

The Message, *The Message* logo, *NavPress*, and the NavPress logo are registered trademarks of NavPress, The Navigators, Colorado Springs, CO. Absence of ® in connection with marks of NavPress or other parties does not indicate an absence of registration of those marks.

Tyndale is a registered trademark of Tyndale House Ministries.

Cover designed by Eva M. Winters

Interior designed by Dean H. Renninger

Cover and interior photograph of rainbow gradient copyright © Sami/Adobe Stock. All rights reserved.

The Message Student Devotional Bible: Psalms is a portion of *The Message: The Bible in Contemporary Language*. It is excerpted from *The Message Student Devotional Bible* (forthcoming).
The Message: The Bible in Contemporary Language copyright © 1993, 2002, 2018 by Eugene H. Peterson. All rights reserved.
The Message: The Bible in Contemporary Language Numbered Edition copyright © 2005.

Published in association with Alive Literary Agency, aliveliterary.com

For information about special discounts for bulk purchases, please contact Tyndale House Publishers at csresponse@tyndale.com, or call 1-855-277-9400.

ISBN 978-1-64158-925-3   Softcover

Printed in China

31	30	29	28	27	26	25
7	6	5	4	3	2	1

CONTENTS

INTRODUCTION TO *THE MESSAGE STUDENT DEVOTIONAL BIBLE*

Let's start with this: The Bible is a really old book. Really, *really* old. Ancient, even. Which is one reason some people ask, "Why should I bother reading the Bible anyway?"

That's a totally fair question. After all, how many other ancient books do you read (besides the ones assigned in school)? Probably not many.

But we believe that the Bible is the most important—and most amazing—book you will ever read because it's so much more than *just* a book. It's actually a collection of books, written by many different people over hundreds of years with lots of different styles and voices, that all together tell one cosmic story of God, the world, humanity, how things were meant to be, how things went wrong, and how God personally stepped into the mess to make things right.

So even though the Bible is an ancient book, the story it tells isn't outdated and will never be outdated, because God doesn't change, human nature doesn't change, and the basic questions that people ask don't change, like these:

Who is God?
What does God have to do with me?
Why is the world such a mess?
Is there hope for the world?
How can I make a difference?
Does my life even matter?
And what about me? Do I matter?

A clarification we should make: The Bible does include a few things that are outdated, like the names of certain towns, the types of money different groups of people used, some cultural laws that were just for a specific time and place, and certain religious practices in the Old Testament you'll go on to see that Jesus fulfilled during his lifetime. But you'll recognize those if you read carefully and thoughtfully. Don't let them distract or bother you. The central story and message of the Bible are clear for anyone with listening ears, an open heart, and an attentive mind.

The most beautiful and compelling thing about the Bible, even the parts that were written before Jesus was born and the parts describing what happened after Jesus left the earth, is that it all points to him—the king of kings, who shows us the heart of God, rescues us from sin, and makes a way for us to have meaningful lives, starting here and now, in relationship with him.

The Bible tells a complete story that runs from Creation (Genesis) to new creation (Revelation). It doesn't include every detail of the story—in fact, John 21:25 says that the world couldn't hold all the books it would take for that—but it does include all the things we need in order to meet, know, and follow the one true God.

The Bible tells an honest story that doesn't avoid or try to clean up all the dark and ugly parts of real history and real people. It's obvious that this isn't a made-up story. Made-up stories are sanitized and spiffed-up. Not the Bible. It's gritty and raw and real.

The Bible tells a clear story that, even if sometimes confusing in small details, is never confusing about the big picture and eternal truth. Thousands of years after it was written, the Bible's imagery and messages still make sense.

The Bible tells a compelling story that draws readers into its surprising turns of events, its portrayal of God's shocking love for people, and its upside-down point of view that exposes the world's foolishness for what it really is.

And the Bible tells a true story that we can trust even as we wrestle with it, believe even as we work to understand it, and follow even as it invites us into a life that is totally counter to what current culture and the world offer.

So we invite you to read the Bible—not in snippets or sound bites, but in chunks that are big enough to teach you, challenge you, and ultimately transform you as its words start to read you back, because that's how powerful and alive this amazing book is.

Those of us who developed this Bible prayed for you as we worked on it. We might not know you by name, but everyone on the team loves Jesus, loves students, and wants you to know deeply how valuable you are. The God who lovingly and intentionally created you wants to meet you in these pages.

MARK OESTREICHER, *founder of The Youth Cartel, author of more than seventy books, and frequent speaker to teenagers, youth workers, and parents*

CRYSTAL KIRGISS, *PhD, director of discipleship content for Young Life, author, and speaker to both teenagers and adults*

. . . and the rest of The Message Student Devotional Bible *team*

HOW TO GET THE MOST OUT OF *THE MESSAGE STUDENT DEVOTIONAL BIBLE*

An amazing pastor, author, and poet named Eugene Peterson spent years translating *The Message,* this version of the Bible. Eugene was passionate about helping people of all ages engage with Scripture, and he believed (like the rest of us on the team who created this student devotional Bible) that, since the Bible is God's primary way of communicating with us, we will grow and learn and live our best lives when we read the Bible.

Throughout history, Christians who wanted to live the fullness of life that Jesus promises us (see John 10:10) have developed regular practices (or habits) of Bible reading.

With all that in mind, here's a little road map of what you'll find in these pages . . .

THE BIBLE ITSELF. This is kind of obvious, right? But we wanted to call it out: The point of all this isn't to create additional stuff you'll read while skipping reading the actual Bible. If you skip all the stuff we created and *only* read the Bible parts, we will still be very, very happy about it. That's first and foremost. Our additional words are *not* the living Word of God; the Bible is.

SECTION INTRODUCTIONS. When reading the Bible, it's helpful to understand what the context and intent are for the various sections it's organized into. In order to help you with that, you'll find six section introductions created by our team that'll help give you some background and landmarks for what each section looks like.

BOOK INTRODUCTIONS. The Bible is *for* you, but it wasn't originally written *to* you. To get the most out of your reading, it's helpful to know who wrote a book of the Bible, who their original audience was, and the context for writing. That's why we've created short book introductions for each of the Bible books (and in a few cases, groups of books). Other than the actual words of Scripture, these might be the next most important thing for you to read.

DEVOTIONS. You'll find 320 devotions spread throughout this Bible. These are intended to help you understand and reflect on God's story and what it means for your life. You'll notice that along with each devo there are three questions. The Bible itself encourages us to meditate on (think about) Scripture, and that's what these questions are designed to help you do. Each devotion has three questions that follow a pattern: (1) a content question, (2) an understanding question, and (3) an application question. Even though they're numbered, the questions in these devos float around on the page. Feel free to go through them sequentially (1, then 2, then 3) or to just start with the question that gets your mind going the fastest. And with all the devotions, you are welcome to work through them in order or jump around—whatever you sense would be helpful to you.

CHARACTER STUDIES. We've often found that the *people* of the Bible have as much for us as the *truths* and *teachings* of the Bible. So, as something of a bonus, there are thirty character studies (fifteen women and fifteen men) at the back of this Bible. They can function like an alternate set of devotions since each also has questions for your reflection.

OTHER HELPFUL STUFF AT THE BACK. Finally, there are a few other helpful things—like an index and some maps of the biblical world—at the very back end.

We hope you're excited to dive into these pages—God is excited to meet you there.

INTRODUCTION TO *THE MESSAGE*

Reading is the first thing, just reading the Bible. As we read we enter a new world of words and find ourselves in on a conversation in which God has the first and last words. We soon realize that we are included in the conversation. We didn't expect this. But this is precisely what generation after generation of Bible readers do find: The Bible is not only written about us but to us. In these pages we become insiders to a conversation in which God uses words to form and bless us, to teach and guide us, to forgive and save us.

We aren't used to this. We are used to reading books that explain things, or tell us what to do, or inspire or entertain us. But this is different. This is a world of revelation: God revealing to people just like us—men and women created in God's image—how God works and what is going on in this world in which we find ourselves. At the same time that God reveals all this, God draws us in by invitation and command to participate in God's working life. We gradually (or suddenly) realize that we are insiders in the most significant action of our time as God establishes his grand rule of love and justice on this earth (as it is in heaven). "Revelation" means that we are reading something we couldn't have guessed or figured out on our own. Revelation is what makes the Bible unique.

And so just reading this Bible, *The Message*, and listening to what we read, is the first thing. There will be time enough for study later on. But first, it is important simply to read, leisurely and thoughtfully. We need to get a feel for the way these stories and songs, these prayers and conversations, these sermons and visions, invite us into this large, large world in which the invisible God is behind and involved in everything visible and illuminates what it means to live here—really live, not just get across the street. As we read, and the longer we read, we begin to "get it"—we are in conversation with God. We find ourselves listening and answering in matters that most concern us: who we are, where we came from, where we are going, what makes us tick, the texture of the world and the communities we live in, and—most of all—the incredible love of God among us, doing for us what we cannot do for ourselves.

Through reading the Bible, we see that there is far more to the world, more to us, more to what we see and more to what we don't see—more to everything!—than we had ever dreamed, and that this "more" has to do with God.

This is new for many of us, a different sort of book—a book that reads us even as we read it. We are used to picking up and reading books for what we can get out of them: information we can use, inspiration to energize us, instructions on how to do something or other, entertainment to while away a rainy day, wisdom that will guide us into living better. These things can and do take place when reading the Bible, but the Bible is given to us in the first place simply to invite us to make ourselves at home in the world of God, God's Word and world, and become familiar with the way God speaks and the ways in which we answer him with our lives.

+ + +

Our reading turns up some surprises. The biggest surprise for many is how accessible this book is to those who simply open it up and read it. Virtually anyone can read this Bible with understanding. The reason that new translations are made every couple of generations or so is to keep the language of the Bible current with the common speech we use, the very language in which it was first written. We don't have to be smart or well-educated to understand it, for it is written in the words and sentences we hear in the marketplace, on school playgrounds, and around the dinner table. Because the Bible is so famous and revered, many assume that we need experts to explain and interpret it for us—and, of course, there are some things that need to be explained. But the first men and women who listened to these words now written in our Bibles were ordinary, everyday, working-class people. One of the greatest of the early translators of the Bible into English, William Tyndale, said that he was translating so that the "boy that driveth the plough" would be able to read the Scriptures.

One well-educated African man, who later became one of the most influential Bible teachers in our history (Augustine), was greatly offended when he first read the Bible. Instead of a book cultivated and polished in the literary style he admired so much, he found it full of homespun, earthy stories of plain, unimportant people. He read it in a Latin translation full of slang and jargon. He took one look at what he considered the "unspiritual" quality of so many of its characters and the everydayness of Jesus, and he contemptuously abandoned it. It was years before he realized that God had not taken the form of a sophisticated intellectual to teach us about highbrow heavenly culture so we could appreciate the finer things of God. When he saw that God entered our lives as a Jewish servant in order to save us from our sins, he started reading the book gratefully and believingly.

Some are also surprised that Bible reading does not introduce us to a "nicer" world. This biblical world is decidedly not an ideal world, the kind we see advertised in travel posters. Suffering and injustice and ugliness are not purged from the world in which God works and loves and saves. Nothing is glossed over. God works patiently and deeply, but often in hidden ways, in the mess of our humanity and history. Ours is not a neat and tidy world in which we are assured that we can get everything under our control. This takes considerable getting used to—there is mystery everywhere. The Bible does not give us a predictable cause-effect world in which we can plan our careers and secure our futures. It is not a dream world in which everything works out according to our adolescent expectations—there is pain and poverty and abuse at which we cry out in indignation, "You can't let this happen!" For most of us it takes years and years and years to exchange our dream world for this real world of grace and mercy, sacrifice and love, freedom and joy—the God-saved world.

Yet another surprise is that the Bible does not flatter us. It is not trying to sell us anything that promises to make life easier. It doesn't offer secrets to what we often think of as prosperity or pleasure or high adventure. The reality that comes into focus as we read the Bible has to do with what God is doing in a saving love that includes us and everything we do. This is quite different from what our sin-stunted and culture-cluttered minds imagine. But our Bible reading does not give us access to a mail-order catalog of idols from which we can pick and choose to satisfy our fantasies. The Bible begins with God speaking creation and us into being. It continues with God entering into personalized and complex relationships with us, helping and blessing us, teaching and training us, correcting and disciplining us, loving and saving us. This is not an escape from reality but a plunge into more reality—a sacrificial but altogether better life all the way.

+ + +

God doesn't force any of this on us: God's Word is personal address, inviting, commanding, challenging, rebuking, judging, comforting, directing—but not forcing. Not coercing. We are given space and freedom to answer, to enter the conversation. For more than anything else the Bible invites our participation in the work and language of God.

As we read, we find that there is a connection between the Word Read and the Word Lived. Everything in this book is live-able. Many of us find that the most important question we ask as we read is not "What does it mean?" but "How can I live it?" So we read personally, not impersonally. We read in order to live our true selves, not just get information that we can use to raise our standard of living. Bible reading is a means of listening to and obeying God, not gathering religious data by which we can be our own gods.

You are going to hear stories in this book that will take you out of your preoccupation with yourself and into the spacious freedom in which God is working the world's salvation. You are going to come across words and sentences that stab you awake to a beauty and hope that will connect you with your real life.

Be sure to answer.

Eugene H. Peterson

INTRODUCTION TO THE WISDOM BOOKS

INFORMATION IS EVERYWHERE. Facts, data, stats, charts—you could spend an entire lifetime gathering information, and while it might make you smart, it won't make you wise. Wisdom is more than just knowledge. Wisdom is deeply rooted in God's good truth, truth that transcends and outlasts today's information.

Wisdom can be found in every book of the Bible, but Job, Psalms, Proverbs, Ecclesiastes, and Song of Songs are thick with wisdom that's delivered in lots of ways, including songs, stories, poems, short sayings, and long teachings. Sometimes the wisdom is obvious right away. Other times it takes some digging to find.

Wisdom can't be read like a report. It's not a one-and-done kind of thing. Wisdom must be savored and digested over and over again so that it seeps into your mind and soul, where it can guide your thoughts, transform your attitudes, and influence your actions.

God's wisdom isn't something that can be boxed up, labeled, set aside, and then opened when needed. It's living and breathing, filled with the Holy Spirit's presence and power, and embodied by Jesus, who *is* God's wisdom (1 Corinthians 1:24).

We all need wisdom. So read it. Savor it. Digest it. And then live it.

INTRODUCTION TO PSALMS

Have you ever felt like you want to say something to God but aren't sure what words to use? Maybe you've even been afraid to say what you're actually thinking, wondering if it's okay to bring your anger or sadness to God. That is one of the most common experiences a Christian can have. And it's why for millennia people have been creating prayer books filled with words we can use to express our hearts to God. But prayer books have another function too: Reading prayers from others helps us learn how to pray ourselves.

That is one of the invitations we find in this book. The book of Psalms is an ancient prayer book in the middle of the Bible. As you read it, you may be surprised by what you find. Some of these prayers would make some church people feel very uncomfortable if a pastor were to stand up and pray them from the pulpit. That's because they aren't just about thanking God for good things; the Psalms are also full of people being completely honest with God. There are times of deep sadness when the writers wonder why they exist and times of intense anger when the writers are shouting at God to annihilate their enemies.

Psalms shows us that all that is fair game in prayer—all that, and a healthy dose of silence and listening too.

1 **1** How well God must like you—
    you don't walk in the ruts of those blind-as-bats,
  you don't stand with the good-for-nothings,
  you don't take your seat among the know-it-alls.

2-3 Instead you thrill to GOD's Word,
    you chew on Scripture day and night.
  You're a tree replanted in Eden,
    bearing fresh fruit every month,
  Never dropping a leaf,
    always in blossom.

4-5 You're not at all like the wicked,
    who are mere windblown dust—
  Without defense in court,
    unfit company for innocent people.

6 GOD charts the road you take.
  The road *they* take leads to nowhere.

1-6 **2** Why the big noise, nations?
    Why the mean plots, peoples?
  Earth-leaders push for position,
  Demagogues and delegates meet for summit talks,
  The God-deniers, the Messiah-defiers:
  "Let's get free of God!
  Cast loose from Messiah!"
  Heaven-throned God breaks out laughing.
  At first he's amused at their presumption;
  Then he gets good and angry.
  Furiously, he shuts them up:
  "Don't you know there's a King in Zion? A coronation banquet
  Is spread for him on the holy summit."

7-9 Let me tell you what GOD said next.
  He said, "You're my son,
  And today is your birthday.
  What do you want? Name it:
  Nations as a present? continents as a prize?
  You can command them all to dance for you,
  Or throw them out with tomorrow's trash."

10-12 So, rebel-kings, use your heads;
  Upstart-judges, learn your lesson:
  Worship GOD in adoring embrace,

There is a difference between liking and loving. This psalm speaks to the good things that God wants us to do and be—the things that God *likes*. These directions help us see a version of ourselves that is good and holy, living well and making the right decisions. The way we experience the life God wants for us is by doing the things God wants us to do. God likes those choices and is happy when we choose them. But they don't make God love us. God loves us no matter what we do. And we can rest in the knowledge that God *loves* us as we try to live in the way God *likes*.

3 Can you think of some other ways God wants you to live well that aren't in this passage?

PSALM 1

What does the phrase "chew on Scripture" (Psalm 1:2) make you think about?
1

2
How does the court metaphor here help you understand the bigger message?

GOD'S LIKE AND GOD'S LOVE

Celebrate in trembling awe. Kiss Messiah!
Your very lives are in danger, you know;
His anger is about to explode,
But if you make a run for God—you won't regret it!

A DAVID PSALM, WHEN HE ESCAPED FOR HIS LIFE FROM ABSALOM, HIS SON

1-2   **3** GOD! Look! Enemies past counting!
      Enemies sprouting like mushrooms,
Mobs of them all around me, roaring their mockery:
"Hah! No help for *him* from God!"

3-4 But you, GOD, shield me on all sides;
You ground my feet, you lift my head high;
With all my might I shout up to GOD,
His answers thunder from the holy mountain.

5-6 I stretch myself out. I sleep.
Then I'm up again—rested, tall and steady,
Fearless before the enemy mobs
Coming at me from all sides.

7 Up, GOD! My God, help me!
Slap their faces,
First this cheek, then the other,
Your fist hard in their teeth!

8 Real help comes from GOD.
Your blessing clothes your people!

A DAVID PSALM

1 **4** When I call, give me answers. God, take my side!
    Once, in a tight place, you gave me room;
Now I'm in trouble again: grace me! hear me!

2 You rabble—how long do I put up with your scorn?
How long will you lust after lies?
How long will you live crazed by illusion?

3 Look at this: look
Who got picked by GOD!
He listens the split second I call to him.

4-5 Complain if you must, but don't lash out.
Keep your mouth shut, and let your heart do the talking.
Build your case before God and wait for his verdict.

6-7 Why is everyone hungry for *more*? "More, more," they say.
"More, more."
I have God's more-than-enough,
More joy in one ordinary day

Than they get in all their shopping sprees.7-8
At day's end I'm ready for sound sleep,
For you, GOD, have put my life back together.

A DAVID PSALM

5 Listen, GOD! Please, pay attention!1-3
    Can you make sense of these ramblings,
  my groans and cries?
  King-God, I need your help.
Every morning
  you'll hear me at it again.
Every morning
  I lay out the pieces of my life
  on your altar
  and watch for fire to descend.

You don't socialize with Wicked,4-6
  or invite Evil over as your houseguest.
Hot-Air-Boaster collapses in front of you;
  you shake your head over Mischief-Maker.
GOD destroys Lie-Speaker;
  Blood-Thirsty and Truth-Bender disgust you.

And here I am, your invited guest—7-8
  it's incredible!
I enter your house; here I am,
  prostrate in your inner sanctum,
Waiting for directions
  to get me safely through enemy lines.

Every word they speak is a land mine;9-10
  their lungs breathe out poison gas.
Their throats are gaping graves,
  their tongues slick as mudslides.
Pile on the guilt, God!
  Let their so-called wisdom wreck them.
Kick them out! They've had their chance.

But you'll welcome us with open arms11-12
  when we run for cover to you.
Let the party last all night!
  Stand guard over our celebration.
You are famous, GOD, for welcoming God-seekers,
  for decking us out in delight.

A DAVID PSALM

6 Please, GOD, no more yelling,1-2
    no more trips to the woodshed.
Treat me nice for a change;
  I'm so starved for affection.

2-3 Can't you see I'm black-and-blue,
     beaten up badly in bones and soul?
GOD, how long will it take
     for you to let up?

4-5 Break in, GOD, and break up this fight;
     if you love me at all, get me out of here.
I'm no good to you dead, am I?
     I can't sing in your choir if I'm buried in
       some tomb!

6-7 I'm tired of all this—so tired. My bed
     has been floating forty days and nights
On the flood of my tears.
     My mattress is soaked, soggy with tears.
The sockets of my eyes are black holes;
     nearly blind, I squint and grope.

8-9 Get out of here, you Devil's crew:
     at last GOD has heard my sobs.
My requests have all been granted,
     my prayers are answered.

10 Cowards, my enemies disappear.
Disgraced, they turn tail and run.

A DAVID PSALM

1-2 **7** GOD! God! I am running to you for dear life;
       the chase is wild.
If they catch me, I'm finished:
     ripped to shreds by foes fierce as lions,
     dragged into the forest and left
     unlooked for, unremembered.

3-5 GOD, if I've done what they say—
     betrayed my friends,
     ripped off my enemies—
If my hands are really that dirty,
     let them get me, walk all over me,
     leave me flat on my face in the dirt.

6-8 Stand up, GOD; pit your holy fury
     against my furious enemies.
Wake up, God. My accusers have packed
     the courtroom; it's judgment time.
Take your place on the bench, reach for
       your gavel,
     throw out the false charges against me.
I'm ready, confident in your verdict:
     "Innocent."

SO TIRED

PSALM 6

1 How and why does this psalm change direction?

Ever been truly exhausted? Not just tired, but so run down and burned out that you lose all sense of perspective? Ever felt like your battery is at one percent and a charger is nowhere to be found? That's how this songwriter feels: beaten up by life, unable to take any more, even starting to blame God. Yet after writing it all out, a thought strikes them: This isn't God's fault at all. God never stopped loving them and has been hearing their prayers. Now the writer turns their focus to their enemies and imagines them scattering away. Sometimes we can lose perspective; talking to God helps us get it back.

2 Which of the emotional phrases in this psalm do you connect with most?

3 The songwriter seems to process their feelings through writing. What would you write to God about what you're feeling?

9-11 Close the book on Evil, GOD,
 but publish your mandate for us.
You get us ready for life:
 you probe for our soft spots,
 you knock off our rough edges.
And I'm feeling so fit, so safe:
 made right, kept right.
God in solemn honor does things right,
 but his nerves are sandpapered raw.

11-13 Nobody gets by with anything.
 God is already in action—
Sword honed on his whetstone,
 bow strung, arrow on the string,
Lethal weapons in hand,
 each arrow a flaming missile.

14 Look at that guy!
 He had sex with sin,
 he's pregnant with evil.
Oh, look! He's having
 the baby—a Lie-Baby!

15-16 See that man shoveling day after day,
 digging, then concealing, his man-trap
 down that lonely stretch of road?
Go back and look again—you'll see him in it headfirst,
 legs waving in the breeze.
That's what happens:
 mischief backfires;
 violence boomerangs.

17 I'm thanking God, who makes things right.
I'm singing the fame of heaven-high GOD.

A DAVID PSALM

1 **8** GOD, brilliant Lord,
 yours is a household name.

2 Nursing infants gurgle choruses about you;
 toddlers shout the songs
That drown out enemy talk,
 and silence atheist babble.

3-4 I look up at your macro-skies, dark and enormous,
 your handmade sky-jewelry,
Moon and stars mounted in their settings.
 Then I look at my micro-self and wonder,
Why do you bother with us?
 Why take a second look our way?

Yet we've so narrowly missed being gods,
    bright with Eden's dawn light.
You put us in charge of your handcrafted world,
    repeated to us your Genesis-charge,
Made us stewards of sheep and cattle,
    even animals out in the wild,
Birds flying and fish swimming,
    whales singing in the ocean deeps.

GOD, brilliant Lord,
    your name echoes around the world.

A DAVID PSALM

9 I'm thanking you, GOD, from a full heart,
    I'm writing the book on your wonders.
I'm whistling, laughing, and jumping for joy;
    I'm singing your song, High God.

The day my enemies turned tail and ran,
    they stumbled on you and fell on their faces.
You took over and set everything right;
    when I needed you, you were there, taking
        charge.

You blow the whistle on godless nations;
    you throw dirty players out of the game,
    wipe their names right off the roster.
Enemies disappear from the sidelines,
    their reputation trashed,
    their names erased from the halls of fame.

GOD holds the high center,
    he sees and sets the world's mess right.
He decides what is right for us earthlings,
    gives people their just deserts.

GOD's a safe-house for the battered,
    a sanctuary during bad times.
The moment you arrive, you relax;
    you're never sorry you knocked.

Sing your songs to Zion-dwelling GOD,
    tell his stories to everyone you meet:
How he tracks down killers
    yet keeps his eye on us,
    registers every whimper and moan.

Be kind to me, GOD;
    I've been kicked around long enough.
Once you've pulled me back
    from the gates of death,

    on the corner of Main and First
    I'll hold a street meeting;
I'll be the song leader; we'll fill the air
    with salvation songs.

15-16 They're trapped, those godless countries,
    in the very snares they set,
Their feet all tangled
    in the net they spread.
They have no excuse;
    the way God works is well-known.
The shrewd machinery made by the wicked
    has maimed their own hands.

17-20 The wicked bought a one-way
    ticket to hell.
No longer will the poor be nameless—
    no more humiliation for the humble.
Up, God! Aren't you fed up with their empty
      strutting?
    Expose these grand pretensions!
Shake them up, God!
    Show them how silly they look.

1-2 **10** God, are you avoiding me?
    Where are you when I need you?
Full of hot air, the wicked
    are hot on the trail of the poor.
Trip them up, tangle them up
    in their fine-tuned plots.

3-4 The wicked are windbags,
    the swindlers have foul breath.
The wicked snub God,
    their noses stuck high in the air.
Their graffiti are scrawled on the walls:
    "Catch us if you can!" "God is dead."

5-6 They care nothing for what you think;
    if you get in their way, they blow you off.
They live (they think) a charmed life:
    "We can't go wrong. This is our lucky year!"

7-8 They carry a mouthful of spells,
    their tongues spit venom like adders.
They hide behind ordinary people,
    then pounce on their victims.

9 They mark the luckless,
    then wait like a hunter in a blind;

When the poor wretch wanders too close,
 they stab him in the back.

The hapless fool is kicked to the ground, 10-11
 the unlucky victim is brutally axed.
He thinks God has dumped him,
 he's sure that God is indifferent to his plight.

Time to get up, GOD—get moving. 12-13
 The luckless think they're Godforsaken.
They wonder why the wicked scorn God
 and get away with it,
Why the wicked are so cocksure
 they'll never come up for audit.

But you know all about it— 14
 the contempt, the abuse.
I dare to believe that the luckless
 will get lucky someday in you.
You won't let them down:
 orphans won't be orphans forever.

Break the wicked right arms, 15-16
 break all the evil left arms.
Search and destroy
 every sign of crime.
GOD's grace and order wins;
 godlessness loses.

The victim's faint pulse picks up; 17-18
 the hearts of the hopeless pump
 red blood
 as you put your ear to their lips.
Orphans get parents,
 the homeless get homes.
The reign of terror is over,
 the rule of the gang lords is ended.

A DAVID PSALM

11 I've already run for dear life 1-3
 straight to the arms of GOD.
So why would I run away now
 when you say,

"Run to the mountains; the evil
 bows are bent, the wicked arrows
Aimed to shoot under cover of darkness
 at every heart open to God.
The bottom's dropped out of the country;
 good people don't have a chance"?

SEARCHING FOR GOD

When you look at the world around you, do you ever feel like it's hard to see where God is amid all the chaos? It's easy to get discouraged and wonder if God sees what's happening. Psalm 10 reminds us that God is always watching over us, even when it doesn't feel like it. The psalmist, or writer of this prayer, cries out to God, asking God to expose the wickedness of those who oppress the innocent. Here's the promise: We are heard and seen, and we can trust that God will bring justice. So let's commit to searching for God and trusting that God is always with us, even in the middle of our darkest moments.

PSALM 10

What examples of wickedness can you think of that make it difficult to see God's presence?

How does the psalmist's cry for justice demonstrate their trust in God's ability to bring about justice?
❷

❸
How can you actively search for and recognize God's presence in your own life, especially during difficult times?

But God hasn't moved to the mountains;   4-6
    his holy address hasn't changed.
He's in charge, as always, his eyes
    taking everything in, his eyelids
Unblinking, examining Adam's flesh and blood
    inside and out, not missing a thing.
He tests the good and the bad alike;
    if anyone cheats, God's outraged.
Fail the test and you're out,
    out in a hail of firestones,
Drinking from a canteen
    filled with hot desert wind.

God's business is putting things right;   7
    he loves getting the lines straight,
Setting us straight. Once we're standing tall,
    we can look him straight in the eye.

A DAVID PSALM

12 Quick, God, I need your helping hand!   1-2
     The last decent person just went down,
All the friends I depended on gone.
Everyone talks in lie language;
Lies slide off their oily lips.
They doubletalk with forked tongues.

Slice their lips off their faces! Pull   3-4
The braggart tongues from their mouths!
I'm tired of hearing, "We can talk anyone into anything!
Our lips manage the world."

Into the hovels of the poor,   5
Into the dark streets where the homeless groan, God speaks:
"I've had enough; I'm on my way
To heal the ache in the heart of the wretched."

God's words are pure words,   6-8
Pure silver words refined seven times
In the fires of his word-kiln,
Pure on earth as well as in heaven.
God, keep us safe from their lies,
From the wicked who stalk us with lies,
From the wicked who collect honors
For their wonderful lies.

A DAVID PSALM

13 Long enough, God—   1-2
     you've ignored me long enough.
I've looked at the back of your head
    long enough. Long enough

I've carried this ton of trouble,
    lived with a stomach full of pain.
Long enough my arrogant enemies
    have looked down their noses at me.

3-4 Take a good look at me, GOD, my God;
    I want to look life in the eye,
So no enemy can get the best of me
    or laugh when I fall on my face.

5-6 I've thrown myself headlong into your
        arms—
    I'm celebrating your rescue.
I'm singing at the top of my lungs,
    I'm so full of answered prayers.

A DAVID PSALM

1 **14** Bilious and bloated, they gas,
        "God is gone."
Their words are poison gas,
    fouling the air; they poison
Rivers and skies;
    thistles are their cash crop.

2 GOD sticks his head out of heaven.
    He looks around.
He's looking for someone not stupid—
    one man, even, God-expectant,
    just one God-ready woman.

3 He comes up empty. A string
    of zeros. Useless, unshepherded
Sheep, taking turns pretending
    to be Shepherd.
The ninety and nine
    follow their fellow.

4 Don't they know anything,
    all these predators?
Don't they know
    they can't get away with this—
Treating people like a fast-food meal
    over which they're too busy to pray?

5-6 Night is coming for them, and nightmares,
    for God takes the side of victims.
Do you think you can mess
    with the dreams of the poor?
You can't, for God
    makes their dreams come true.

Is there anyone around to save Israel?   7
   Yes. God is around; GOD turns life around.
Turned-around Jacob skips rope,
   turned-around Israel sings laughter.

A DAVID PSALM

15 GOD, who gets invited   1
    to dinner at your place?
How do we get on your guest list?

"Walk straight,   2
   act right,
      tell the truth.

"Don't hurt your friend,   3-4
   don't blame your neighbor;
      despise the despicable.

"Keep your word even when it costs you,   5
   make an honest living,
      never take a bribe.

"You'll never get
blacklisted
if you live like this."

A DAVID SONG

16 Keep me safe, O God,   1-2
    I've run for dear life to you.
I say to GOD, "Be my Lord!"
   Without you, nothing makes sense.

And these God-chosen lives all around—   3
   what splendid friends they make!

Don't just go shopping for a god.   4
   Gods are not for sale.
I swear I'll never treat god-names
   like brand-names.

My choice is you, GOD, first and only.   5-6
   And now I find I'm *your* choice!
You set me up with a house and yard.
   And then you made me your heir!

The wise counsel GOD gives when I'm awake   7-8
   is confirmed by my sleeping heart.
Day and night I'll stick with GOD;
   I've got a good thing going and I'm not
      letting go.

WALK STRAIGHT, ACT RIGHT, TELL THE TRUTH

Living a life of faith isn't always complicated. In terms of what God actually requires from us, sometimes it's much simpler than we think. Although the Bible contains a lot of guidelines for living, they really all point to the same ideas. First, choosing to walk through life with God: putting God first and doing everything *with*—instead of *without*—God. Second, doing the things that God would want: making sure our actions reflect our faith. Third, making sure our words are honest, are good, and have integrity. If we focus on these three principles, everything else will follow.

3 What does it look like to "walk straight," "act right," and "tell the truth" (Psalm 15:2) in your life right now? What might need to change?

How does the psalmist illustrate what these rules for living look like in practice?

1

PSALM 15

Why are these three guiding principles so important to God?

2

I'm happy from the inside out,   9-10
    and from the outside in, I'm firmly formed.
You canceled my ticket to hell—
    that's not my destination!

Now you've got my feet on the life path,   11
    all radiant from the shining of your face.
Ever since you took my hand,
    I'm on the right way.

A DAVID PRAYER

17 Listen while I build my case, GOD,   1-2
    the most honest prayer you'll ever hear.
Show the world I'm innocent—
    in your heart you know I am.

Go ahead, examine me from inside out,   3
    surprise me in the middle of the night—
You'll find I'm just what I say I am.
    My words don't run loose.

I'm not trying to get my way   4-5
    in the world's way.
I'm trying to get *your* way,
    your Word's way.
I'm staying on your trail;
    I'm putting one foot
In front of the other.
    I'm not giving up.

I call to you, God, because I'm sure of an answer.   6-7
    So—answer! bend your ear! listen sharp!
Paint grace-graffiti on the fences;
    take in your frightened children who
Are running from the neighborhood bullies
    straight to you.

Keep your eye on me;   8-9
    hide me under your cool wing feathers
From the wicked who are out to get me,
    from mortal enemies closing in.

Their hearts are hard as nails,   10-14
    their mouths blast hot air.
They are after me, nipping my heels,
    determined to bring me down,
Lions ready to rip me apart,
    young lions poised to pounce.
Up, GOD: beard them! break them!
    By your sword, free me from their clutches;

Barehanded, GOD, break these mortals,
   these flat-earth people who can't think
      beyond today.

I'd like to see their bellies
   swollen with famine food,
The weeds they've sown
   harvested and baked into famine bread,
With second helpings for their children
   and crusts for their babies to chew on.

15 And me? I plan on looking
   you full in the face. When I get up,
I'll see your full stature
   and live heaven on earth.

**A DAVID SONG, WHICH HE SANG TO GOD AFTER BEING SAVED
FROM ALL HIS ENEMIES AND FROM SAUL**

1-2 **18** I love you, GOD—
      you make me strong.
GOD is bedrock under my feet,
   the castle in which I live,
   my rescuing knight.
My God—the high crag
   where I run for dear life,
   hiding behind the boulders,
   safe in the granite hideout.

3 I sing to GOD, the Praise-Lofty,
   and find myself safe and saved.

4-5 The hangman's noose was tight at my throat;
   devil waters rushed over me.
Hell's ropes cinched me tight;
   death traps barred every exit.

6 A hostile world! I call to GOD,
   I cry to God to help me.
From his palace he hears my call;
   my cry brings me right into his presence—
   a private audience!

7-15 Earth wobbles and lurches;
   huge mountains shake like leaves,
Quake like aspen leaves
   because of his rage.
His nostrils flare, bellowing smoke;
   his mouth spits fire.
Tongues of fire dart in and out;
   he lowers the sky.

He steps down;
    under his feet an abyss opens up.
He's riding a winged creature,
    swift on wind-wings.
Now he's wrapped himself
    in a trenchcoat of black-cloud darkness.
But his cloud-brightness bursts through,
    spraying hailstones and fireballs.
Then GOD thundered out of heaven;
    the High God gave a great shout,
    spraying hailstones and fireballs.
God shoots his arrows—pandemonium!
    He hurls his lightnings—a rout!
The secret sources of ocean are exposed,
    the hidden depths of earth lie uncovered
The moment you roar in protest,
    let loose your hurricane anger.

But me he caught—reached all the way   16-19
    from sky to sea; he pulled me out
Of that ocean of hate, that enemy chaos,
    the void in which I was drowning.
They hit me when I was down,
    but GOD stuck by me.
He stood me up on a wide-open field;
    I stood there saved—surprised to be loved!

GOD made my life complete   20-24
    when I placed all the pieces before him.
When I got my act together,
    he gave me a fresh start.
Now I'm alert to GOD's ways;
    I don't take God for granted.
Every day I review the ways he works;
    I try not to miss a trick.
I feel put back together,
    and I'm watching my step.
GOD rewrote the text of my life
    when I opened the book of my heart to his eyes.

The good people taste your goodness,   25-27
The whole people taste your health,
The true people taste your truth,
The bad ones can't figure you out.
You take the side of the down-and-out,
But the stuck-up you take down a notch.

Suddenly, GOD, you floodlight my life;   28-29
    I'm blazing with glory, God's glory!
I smash the bands of marauders,
    I vault the highest fences.

30 What a God! His road
    stretches straight and smooth.
  Every GOD-direction is road-tested.
    Everyone who runs toward him
  Makes it.

31-42 Is there any god like GOD?
    Are we not at bedrock?
  Is not this the God who armed me,
    then aimed me in the right direction?
  Now I run like a deer;
    I'm king of the mountain.
  He shows me how to fight;
    I can bend a bronze bow!
  You protect me with salvation-armor;
    you hold me up with a firm hand,
    caress me with your gentle ways.
  You cleared the ground under me
    so my footing was firm.
  When I chased my enemies I caught them;
    I didn't let go till they were dead men.
  I nailed them; they were down for good;
    then I walked all over them.
  You armed me well for this fight,
    you smashed the upstarts.
  You made my enemies turn tail,
    and I wiped out the haters.
  They cried "uncle"
    but Uncle didn't come;
  They yelled for GOD
    and got no for an answer.
  I ground them to dust; they gusted in the wind.
    I threw them out, like garbage in the gutter.

43-45 You rescued me from a squabbling people;
    you made me a leader of nations.
  People I'd never heard of served me;
    the moment they got wind of me they listened.
  The foreign devils gave up; they came
    on their bellies, crawling from their hideouts.

46-48 Live, GOD! Blessings from my Rock,
    my free and freeing God, towering!
  This God set things right for me
    and shut up the people who talked back.
  He rescued me from enemy anger,
    he pulled me from the grip of upstarts,
  He saved me from the bullies.

49-50 That's why I'm thanking you, GOD,
    all over the world.

That's why I'm singing songs
    that rhyme your name.
God's king takes the trophy;
    God's chosen is beloved.
I mean David and all his children—
    always.

A DAVID PSALM

19 God's glory is on tour in the skies,   1-2
    God-craft on exhibit across the horizon.
Madame Day holds classes every morning,
    Professor Night lectures each evening.

Their words aren't heard,   3-4
    their voices aren't recorded,
But their silence fills the earth:
    unspoken truth is spoken everywhere.

God makes a huge dome   4-5
    for the sun—a superdome!
The morning sun's a new husband
    leaping from his honeymoon bed,
The daybreaking sun an athlete
    racing to the tape.

That's how God's Word vaults across the skies   6
    from sunrise to sunset,
Melting ice, scorching deserts,
    warming hearts to faith.

The revelation of GOD is whole   7-9
    and pulls our lives together.
The signposts of GOD are clear
    and point out the right road.
The life-maps of GOD are right,
    showing the way to joy.
The directions of GOD are plain
    and easy on the eyes.
GOD's reputation is twenty-four-carat gold,
    with a lifetime guarantee.
The decisions of GOD are accurate
    down to the nth degree.

God's Word is better than a diamond,   10
    better than a diamond set between emeralds.
You'll like it better than strawberries in spring,
    better than red, ripe strawberries.

There's more: God's Word warns us of danger   11-14
    and directs us to hidden treasure.

Otherwise how will we find our way?
  Or know when we play the fool?
Clean the slate, God, so we can start the
    day fresh!
  Keep me from stupid sins,
  from thinking I can take over your work;
Then I can start this day sun-washed,
  scrubbed clean of the grime of sin.
These are the words in my mouth;
  these are what I chew on and pray.
Accept them when I place them
  on the morning altar,
O God, my Altar-Rock,
  God, Priest-of-My-Altar.

A DAVID PSALM

1-4 **20** GOD answer you on the day you crash,
    The name God-of-Jacob put you out of harm's reach,
Send reinforcements from Holy Hill,
Dispatch from Zion fresh supplies,
Exclaim over your offerings,
Celebrate your sacrifices,
Give you what your heart desires,
Accomplish your plans.

5 When you win, we plan to raise the roof
    and lead the parade with our banners.
  May all your wishes come true!

6 That clinches it—help's coming,
    an answer's on the way,
      everything's going to work out.

7-8 See those people polishing their chariots,
    and those others grooming their horses?
      But we're making garlands for GOD our God.
  The chariots will rust,
    those horses pull up lame—
      and we'll be on our feet, standing tall.

9 Make the king a winner, GOD;
    the day we call, give us your answer.

A DAVID PSALM

1-7 **21** Your strength, GOD, is the king's strength.
    Helped, he's hollering Hosannas.
You gave him exactly what he wanted;
  you didn't hold back.
You filled his arms with gifts;
  you gave him a right royal welcome.

He wanted a good life; you gave it to him,
    and then made it a *long* life as a bonus.
You lifted him high and bright as a cumulus cloud,
    then dressed him in rainbow colors.
You pile blessings on him;
    you make him glad when you smile.
Is it any wonder the king loves GOD?
    that he's sticking with the Best?

With a fistful of enemies in one hand   8-12
    and a fistful of haters in the other,
You radiate with such brilliance
    that they cringe as before a furnace.
Now the furnace swallows them whole,
    the fire eats them alive!
You purge the earth of their progeny,
    you wipe the slate clean.
All their evil schemes, the plots they cook up,
    have fizzled—every one.
You sent them packing;
    they couldn't face you.

Show your strength, GOD, so no one can miss it.   13
    We are out singing the good news!

A DAVID PSALM

22 God, God . . . my God!   1-2
    Why did you dump me
miles from nowhere?
Doubled up with pain, I call to God
    all the day long. No answer. Nothing.
I keep at it all night, tossing and turning.

And you! Are you indifferent, above it all,   3-5
    leaning back on the cushions of Israel's praise?
We know you were there for our parents:
    they cried for your help and you gave it;
    they trusted and lived a good life.

And here I am, a nothing—an earthworm,   6-8
    something to step on, to squash.
Everyone pokes fun at me;
    they make faces at me, they shake their heads:
"Let's see how GOD handles this one;
    since God likes him so much, let *him* help him!"

And to think you were midwife at my birth,   9-11
    setting me at my mother's breasts!
When I left the womb you cradled me;
    since the moment of birth you've been my God.

Then you moved far away
    and trouble moved in next door.
I need a neighbor.

12-13   Herds of bulls come at me,
    the raging bulls stampede,
Horns lowered, nostrils flaring,
    like a herd of buffalo on the move.

14-15   I'm a bucket kicked over and spilled,
    every joint in my body has been pulled apart.
My heart is a blob
    of melted wax in my gut.
I'm dry as a bone,
    my tongue black and swollen.
They have laid me out for burial
    in the dirt.

16-18   Now packs of wild dogs come at me;
    thugs gang up on me.
They pin me down hand and foot,
    and lock me in a cage—a bag
Of bones in a cage, stared at
    by every passerby.
They take my wallet and the shirt off my back,
    and then throw dice for my clothes.

19-21   You, GOD—don't put off my rescue!
    Hurry and help me!
Don't let them cut my throat;
    don't let those mongrels devour me.
If you don't show up soon,
    I'm done for—gored by the bulls,
    meat for the lions.

22-24   Here's the story I'll tell my friends when they come to worship,
    and punctuate it with Hallelujahs:
Shout Hallelujah, you God-worshipers;
    give glory, you sons of Jacob;
    adore him, you daughters of Israel.
He has never let you down,
    never looked the other way
    when you were being kicked around.
He has never wandered off to do his own thing;
    he has been right there, listening.

25-26   Here in this great gathering for worship
    I have discovered this praise-life.
And I'll do what I promised right here
    in front of the God-worshipers.

A DAVID PSALM IN THE MOUTH OF JESUS

1
Why do you think David feels abandoned by God?

"God, God . . . my God! Why did you dump me miles from nowhere?" These words (often translated "My God, my God, why have you abandoned me?") are David's opening words in Psalm 22. They're a cry of abandonment, yelled as David is "doubled up with pain," crying out to God but hearing nothing in return (Psalm 22:1-2). What's remarkable about this psalm isn't just that David utters these words to an all-powerful God. It's also that, centuries later, Jesus uses these words to cry out to God as he's dying on the cross (see Matthew 27:46 and Mark 15:34). Like David, Jesus hears nothing from God but cries out anyway, confident that God is listening. We can be just as confident that God is always listening to us, even when we hear nothing in response.

PSALM 22

How does it make you feel to know that God is always listening, even when you hear nothing in response?

3

2 What might contribute to Jesus' confidence that God is listening to him—even though God doesn't respond in the way we might expect?

Down-and-outers sit at GOD's table
    and eat their fill.
Everyone on the hunt for God
    is here, praising him.
"Live it up, from head to toe.
    Don't ever quit!"

27-28   From the four corners of the earth
    people are coming to their senses,
    are running back to GOD.
Long-lost families
    are falling on their faces before him.
GOD has taken charge;
    from now on he has the last word.

29   All the power-mongers are before him
    —worshiping!
All the poor and powerless, too
    —worshiping!
Along with those who never got it together
    —worshiping!

30-31   Our children and their children
    will get in on this
As the word is passed along
    from parent to child.
Babies not yet conceived
    will hear the good news—
    that God does what he says.

A DAVID PSALM

1-3   **23**   GOD, my shepherd!
    I don't need a thing.
You have bedded me down in lush
    meadows,
    you find me quiet pools to drink from.
True to your word,
    you let me catch my breath
    and send me in the right direction.

4   Even when the way goes through
    Death Valley,
I'm not afraid
    when you walk at my side.
Your trusty shepherd's crook
    makes me feel secure.

5   You serve me a six-course dinner
    right in front of my enemies.
You revive my drooping head;
    my cup brims with blessing.

Your beauty and love chase after me   6
    every day of my life.
I'm back home in the house of GOD
    for the rest of my life.

A DAVID PSALM

24 GOD claims Earth and everything in it,   1-2
       GOD claims World and all who live on it.
He built it on Ocean foundations,
    laid it out on River girders.

Who can climb Mount GOD?   3-4
    Who can scale the holy north-face?
Only the clean-handed,
    only the pure-hearted;
Men who won't cheat,
    women who won't seduce.

GOD is at their side;   5-6
    with GOD's help they make it.
This, Jacob, is what happens
    to God-seekers, God-questers.

Wake up, you sleepyhead city!   7
Wake up, you sleepyhead people!
    King-Glory is ready to enter.

Who is this King-Glory?   8
    GOD, armed
    and battle-ready.

Wake up, you sleepyhead city!   9
Wake up, you sleepyhead people!
    King-Glory is ready to enter.

Who is this King-Glory?   10
    GOD-of-the-Angel-Armies:
    he is King-Glory.

A DAVID PSALM

25 My head is high, GOD, held high;   1-2
       I'm looking to you, GOD;
No hangdog skulking for me.

I've thrown in my lot with you;   3
You won't embarrass me, will you?
Or let my enemies get the best of me?

Don't embarrass any of us
Who went out on a limb for you.
It's the traitors who should be humiliated.

4   Show me how you work, GOD;
    School me in your ways.

5   Take me by the hand;
    Lead me down the path of truth.
    You are my Savior, aren't you?

6   Mark the milestones of your mercy and love, GOD;
    Rebuild the ancient landmarks!

7   Forget that I sowed wild oats;
    Mark me with your sign of love.
    Plan only the best for me, GOD!

8   GOD is fair and just;
    He corrects the misdirected,
    Sends them in the right direction.

9   He gives the rejects his hand,
    And leads them step-by-step.

10 From now on every road you travel
    Will take you to GOD.
    Follow the Covenant signs;
    Read the charted directions.

11 Keep up your reputation, GOD;
    Forgive my bad life;
    It's been a very bad life.

12 My question: What are God-worshipers like?
    Your answer: Arrows aimed at God's bull's-eye.

13 They settle down in a promising place;
    Their kids inherit a prosperous farm.

14 God-friendship is for God-worshipers;
    They are the ones he confides in.

15 If I keep my eyes on GOD,
    I won't trip over my own feet.

16 Look at me and help me!
    I'm all alone and in big trouble.

17 My heart and mind are fighting each other;
    Call a truce to this civil war.

18 Take a hard look at my life of hard labor,
    Then lift this ton of sin.

Do you see how many people   19
Have it in for me?
How viciously they hate me?

Keep watch over me and keep me out of trouble;   20
Don't let me down when I run to you.

Use all your skill to put me together;   21
I wait to see your finished product.

GOD, give your people a break   22
From this run of bad luck.

A DAVID PSALM
26
Clear my name, GOD;   1
   I've kept an honest shop.
I've thrown in my lot with you, GOD, and
   I'm not budging.

Examine me, GOD, from head to foot,   2
   order your battery of tests.
Make sure I'm fit
   inside and out

So I never lose   3
   sight of your love,
But keep in step with you,
   never missing a beat.

I don't hang out with tricksters,   4-5
   I don't pal around with thugs;
I hate that pack of gangsters,
   I don't deal with double-dealers.

I scrub my hands with purest soap,   6-7
   then join hands with the others in the
      great circle,
   dancing around your altar, GOD,
Singing God-songs at the top of my lungs,
   telling God-stories.

GOD, I love living with you;   8-10
   your house glows with your glory.
When it's time for spring cleaning,
   don't sweep me out with the quacks and crooks,
Men with bags of dirty tricks,
   women with purses stuffed with bribe-money.

You know I've been aboveboard with you;   11-12
   now be aboveboard with me.

I'm on the level with you, GOD;
    I bless you every chance I get.

A DAVID PSALM

1 **27** Light, space, zest—
        that's GOD!
So, with him on my side I'm fearless,
    afraid of no one and nothing.

2 When vandal hordes ride down
    ready to eat me alive,
Those bullies and toughs
    fall flat on their faces.

3 When besieged,
    I'm calm as a baby.
When all hell breaks loose,
    I'm collected and cool.

4 I'm asking GOD for one thing,
    only one thing:
To live with him in his house
    my whole life long.
I'll contemplate his beauty;
    I'll study at his feet.

5 That's the only quiet, secure place
    in a noisy world,
The perfect getaway,
    far from the buzz of traffic.

6 God holds me head and shoulders
    above all who try to pull me down.
I'm headed for his place to offer anthems
    that will raise the roof!
Already I'm singing God-songs;
    I'm making music to GOD.

7-9 Listen, GOD, I'm calling at the top of
      my lungs:
    "Be good to me! Answer me!"
When my heart whispered, "Seek God,"
    my whole being replied,
"I'm seeking him!"
    Don't hide from me now!

9-10 You've always been right there for me;
    don't turn your back on me now.
Don't throw me out, don't abandon me;
    you've always kept the door open.

My father and mother walked out and
    left me,
  but GOD took me in.

Point me down your highway, GOD;   11-12
  direct me along a well-lighted street;
  show my enemies whose side
    you're on.
Don't throw me to the dogs,
  those liars who are out to get me,
  filling the air with their threats.

I'm sure now I'll see God's goodness   13-14
  in the exuberant earth.
Stay with GOD!
  Take heart. Don't quit.
I'll say it again:
  Stay with GOD.

A DAVID PSALM

28 Don't turn a deaf ear   1
    when I call you, GOD.
If all I get from you is
  deafening silence,
I'd be better off
  in the Black Hole.

I'm letting you know what I need,   2
  calling out for help
And lifting my arms
  toward your inner sanctuary.

Don't shove me into   3-4
  the same jail cell with those crooks,
With those who are
  full-time employees of evil.
They talk a good line of "peace,"
  then moonlight for the Devil.

Pay them back for what they've done,
  for how bad they've been.
Pay them back for their long hours
  in the Devil's workshop;
Then cap it with a huge bonus.

Because they have no idea how   5
    God works
  or what he is up to,
God will smash them to smithereens
  and walk away from the ruins.

6-7 Blessed be GOD—
> he heard me praying.
> He proved he's on my side;
>> I've thrown my lot in with him.

> Now I'm jumping for joy,
>> and shouting and singing my thanks to him.

8-9 GOD is all strength for his people,
>> ample refuge for his chosen leader;
> Save your people
>> and bless your heritage.
> Care for them;
>> carry them like a good shepherd.

A DAVID PSALM

1-2 **29** Bravo, GOD, bravo!
>> Gods and all angels shout, "Encore!"
> In awe before the glory,
>> in awe before God's visible power.
> Stand at attention!
>> Dress your best to honor him!

3 GOD thunders across the waters,
> Brilliant, his voice and his face, streaming brightness—
> GOD, across the flood waters.

4 GOD's thunder tympanic,
> GOD's thunder symphonic.

5 GOD's thunder smashes cedars,
> GOD topples the northern cedars.

6 The mountain ranges skip like spring colts,
> The high ridges jump like wild kid goats.

7-8 GOD's thunder spits fire.
> GOD thunders, the wilderness quakes;
> He makes the desert of Kadesh shake.

9 GOD's thunder sets the oak trees dancing
> A wild dance, whirling; the pelting rain strips
>> their branches.
> We fall to our knees—we call out, "Glory!"

10 Above the floodwaters is GOD's throne
>> from which his power flows,
>> from which he rules the world.

11 GOD makes his people strong.
> GOD gives his people peace.

UNHEARD BY GOD

❷ What does it mean to trust that God is your strength and refuge, especially when it feels like your prayers are unanswered?

It can be frustrating to feel like our problems are going unheard by God. This psalmist lands on a powerful realization: God is our strength and refuge, and we can trust in God completely. We can come to God with our problems and pour out our hearts; but we have to remain steadfast in our faith even when it feels like our prayers are unanswered. God is always with us, and God will never abandon us. Let's hold on to that truth and continue to pray, trusting that God *does* hear us and will give us peace and love.

PSALM 28

How is the psalmist's cry for help relatable to your own experiences? ❶

❸ What's one way you can actively remind yourself to hold on to the truth that God is always with you, even when you face challenges?

A DAVID PSALM

30 ¹ I give you all the credit, GOD—
    you got me out of that mess,
  you didn't let my foes gloat.

2-3 GOD, my God, I yelled for help
      and you put me together.
   GOD, you pulled me out of the grave,
      gave me another chance at life
      when I was down-and-out.

4-5 All you saints! Sing your hearts out to GOD!
      Thank him to his face!
   He gets angry once in a while, but across
      a lifetime there is only love.
   The nights of crying your eyes out
      give way to days of laughter.

6-7 When things were going great
      I crowed, "I've got it made.
   I'm GOD's favorite.
      He made me king of the mountain."
   Then you looked the other way
      and I fell to pieces.

8-10 I called out to you, GOD;
      I laid my case before you:
   "Can you sell me for a profit when I'm dead?
      auction me off at a cemetery yard sale?
   When I'm 'dust to dust' my songs
      and stories of you won't sell.
   So listen! and be kind!
      Help me out of this!"

11-12 You did it: you changed wild lament
      into whirling dance;
   You ripped off my black mourning band
      and decked me with wildflowers.
   I'm about to burst with song;
      I can't keep quiet about you.
   GOD, my God,
      I can't thank you enough.

A DAVID PSALM

31 ¹⁻² I run to you, GOD; I run for dear life.
       Don't let me down!
    Take me seriously this time!
   Get down on my level and listen,
      and please—no procrastination!
   Your granite cave a hiding place,
      your high cliff nest a place of safety.

You're my cave to hide in,   3-5
   my cliff to climb.
Be my safe leader,
   be my true mountain guide.
Free me from hidden traps;
   I want to hide in you.
I've put my life in your hands.
   You won't drop me,
   you'll never let me down.

I hate all this silly religion,   6-13
   but you, GOD, I trust.
I'm leaping and singing in the circle of your love;
   you saw my pain,
   you disarmed my tormentors,
You didn't leave me in their clutches
   but gave me room to breathe.
Be kind to me, GOD—
   I'm in deep, deep trouble again.
I've cried my eyes out;
   I feel hollow inside.
My life leaks away, groan by groan;
   my years fade out in sighs.
My troubles have worn me out,
   turned my bones to powder.
To my enemies I'm a monster;
   I'm ridiculed by the neighbors.
My friends are horrified;
   they cross the street to avoid me.
They want to blot me from memory,
   forget me like a corpse in a grave,
   discard me like a broken dish in the trash.
The street-talk gossip has me
   "criminally insane"!
Behind locked doors they plot
   how to ruin me for good.

Desperate, I throw myself on you: 14-18
   you are my God!
Hour by hour I place my days in your hand,
   safe from the hands out to get me.
Warm me, your servant, with a smile;
   save me because you love me.
Don't embarrass me by not showing up;
   I've given you plenty of notice.
Embarrass the wicked, stand them up,
   leave them stupidly shaking their heads
   as they drift down to hell.
Gag those loudmouthed liars
   who heckle me, your follower,
   with jeers and catcalls.

19-22　What a stack of blessing you have piled up
　　　　for those who worship you,
　　　Ready and waiting for all who run to you
　　　　to escape an unkind world.
　　　You hide them safely away
　　　　from the opposition.
　　　As you slam the door on those oily, mocking faces,
　　　　you silence the poisonous gossip.
　　　Blessed GOD!
　　　　His love is the wonder of the world.
　　　Trapped by a siege, I panicked.
　　　　"Out of sight, out of mind," I said.
　　　But you heard me say it,
　　　　you heard and listened.

23　　Love GOD, all you saints;
　　　　GOD takes care of all who stay close to him,
　　　But he pays back in full
　　　　those arrogant enough to go it alone.

24　　Be brave. Be strong. Don't give up.
　　　　Expect GOD to get here soon.

A DAVID PSALM

1　**32**　Count yourself lucky, how happy you must be—
　　　　　you get a fresh start,
　　　your slate's wiped clean.

2　　Count yourself lucky—
　　　　GOD holds nothing against you
　　　　and you're holding nothing back from him.

3　　When I kept it all inside,
　　　　my bones turned to powder,
　　　　my words became daylong groans.

4　　The pressure never let up;
　　　　all the juices of my life dried up.

5　　Then I let it all out;
　　　　I said, "I'll come clean about my failures
　　　　　to GOD."

　　　Suddenly the pressure was gone—
　　　　my guilt dissolved,
　　　　my sin disappeared.

6　　These things add up. Every one of us needs
　　　　to pray;
　　　　when all hell breaks loose and the dam bursts
　　　　we'll be on high ground, untouched.

God's my island hideaway,
   keeps danger far from the shore,
   throws garlands of hosannas around my neck.

7

Let me give you some good advice;
   I'm looking you in the eye
   and giving it to you straight:

8

"Don't be ornery like a horse or mule
   that needs bit and bridle
   to stay on track."

9

God-defiers are always in trouble;
   God-affirmers find themselves loved
   every time they turn around.

10

Celebrate God.
   Sing together—everyone!
   All you honest hearts, raise the roof!

11

33 Good people, cheer God!
   Right-living people sound best when praising.
Use guitars to reinforce your Hallelujahs!
   Play his praise on a grand piano!
Compose your own new song to him;
   give him a trumpet fanfare.

1-3

For God's Word is solid to the core;
   everything he makes is sound inside and out.
He loves it when everything fits,
   when his world is in plumb-line true.
Earth is drenched
   in God's affectionate satisfaction.

4-5

The skies were made by God's command;
   he breathed the word and the stars popped out.
He scooped Sea into his jug,
   put Ocean in his keg.

6-7

Earth-creatures, bow before God;
   world-dwellers—down on your knees!
Here's why: he spoke and there it was,
   in place the moment he said so.

8-9

God takes the wind out of Babel pretense,
   he shoots down the world's power-schemes.
God's plan for the world stands up,
   all his designs are made to last.
Blessed is the country with God for God;
   blessed are the people he's put in his will.

10-12

13-15 From high in the skies GOD looks around,
   he sees all Adam's brood.
From where he sits
   he overlooks all us earth-dwellers.
He has shaped each person in turn;
   now he watches everything we do.

16-17 No king succeeds with a big army alone,
   no warrior wins by brute strength.
Horsepower is not the answer;
   no one gets by on muscle alone.

18-19 Watch this: God's eye is on those who respect him,
   the ones who are looking for his love.
He's ready to come to their rescue in bad times;
   in lean times he keeps body and soul together.

20-22 We're depending on GOD;
   he's everything we need.
What's more, our hearts brim with joy
   since we've taken for our own his holy name.
Love us, GOD, with all you've got—
   that's what we're depending on.

A DAVID PSALM, WHEN HE OUTWITTED ABIMELECH AND GOT AWAY

1 **34** I bless GOD every chance I get;
   my lungs expand with his praise.

2 I live and breathe GOD;
   if things aren't going well, hear this and be happy:

3 Join me in spreading the news;
   together let's get the word out.

4 GOD met me more than halfway,
   he freed me from my anxious fears.

5 Look at him; give him your warmest smile.
   Never hide your feelings from him.

6 When I was desperate, I called out,
   and GOD got me out of a tight spot.

7 GOD's angel sets up a circle
   of protection around us while we pray.

8 Open your mouth and taste, open your eyes
      and see—
   how good GOD is.
Blessed are you who run to him.

Worship God if you want the best;
worship opens doors to all his goodness.

9

Young lions on the prowl get hungry,
but God-seekers are full of God.

10

Come, children, listen closely;
I'll give you a lesson in God worship.

11

Who out there has a lust for life?
Can't wait each day to come upon beauty?

12

Guard your tongue from profanity,
and no more lying through your teeth.

13

Turn your back on sin; do something good.
Embrace peace—don't let it get away!

14

God keeps an eye on his friends,
his ears pick up every moan and groan.

15

God won't put up with rebels;
he'll cull them from the pack.

16

Is anyone crying for help? God is listening,
ready to rescue you.

17

If your heart is broken, you'll find God right there;
if you're kicked in the gut, he'll help you catch your breath.

18

Disciples so often get into trouble;
still, God is there every time.

19

He's your bodyguard, shielding every bone;
not even a finger gets broken.

20

The wicked commit slow suicide;
they waste their lives hating the good.

21

God pays for each slave's freedom;
no one who runs to him loses out.

22

A DAVID PSALM

35 Harass these hecklers, God,
punch these bullies in the nose.
Grab a weapon, anything at hand;
stand up for me!
Get ready to throw the spear, aim the javelin,
at the people who are out to get me.
Reassure me; let me hear you say,
"I'll save you."

1-3

Let's be honest: It's not easy to be grateful in difficult times. (We also don't always remember to give thanks when things are going really well!) In this psalm, David is giving thanks for God's deliverance from a very dangerous and difficult situation. He's not completely out of the woods yet, but he recognizes and acknowledges God's presence and deliverance in the midst of what he's going through. The ability to give thanks while we're in tough, challenging, or even dangerous situations allows us to grow closer to God and reminds us that God is with us every moment and in every context.

PSALM 34

① Where do you notice David shift between talking about the joy and hope of God and the reality of oppression and hurt?

② How does David talk about who God is and about God's character?

③ What could you do, say, or think about a difficult situation in your own life to help you experience God's presence with you in the midst of it?

GOD IS THERE

EVERY TIME

When those thugs try to knife me in the back,
  make them look foolish.
Frustrate all those
  who are plotting my downfall.
Make them like cinders in a high wind,
  with GOD's angel working the bellows.
Make their road lightless and mud-slick,
  with GOD's angel on their tails.
Out of sheer cussedness they set a trap to catch me;
  for no good reason they dug a ditch to stop me.
Surprise them with your ambush—
  catch them in the very trap they set,
  the disaster they planned for me.

But let me run loose and free,
  celebrating GOD's great work,
Every bone in my body laughing, singing, "GOD,
  there's no one like you.
You put the down-and-out on their feet
  and protect the unprotected from bullies!"

Hostile accusers appear out of nowhere,
  they stand up and badger me.
They pay me back misery for mercy,
  leaving my soul empty.

When they were sick, I dressed in black;
  instead of eating, I prayed.
My prayers were like lead in my gut,
  like I'd lost my best friend, my brother.
I paced, distraught as a motherless child,
  hunched and heavyhearted.

But when I was down
  they threw a party!
All the nameless misfits of the town came
  chanting insults about me.
Like barbarians desecrating a shrine,
  they destroyed my reputation.

GOD, how long are you going
  to stand there doing nothing?
Save me from their brutalities;
  everything I've got is being thrown to the lions.
I will give you full credit
  when everyone gathers for worship;
When the people turn out in force
  I will say my Hallelujahs.

Don't let these liars, my enemies,
  have a party at my expense,

Those who hate me for no reason,
   winking and rolling their eyes.
No good is going to come
   from that crowd;
They spend all their time cooking up gossip
   against those who mind their own business.
They open their mouths
   in ugly grins,
Mocking, "Ha-ha, ha-ha, thought you'd get away
     with it?
   We've caught you hands down!"

22 Don't you see what they're doing, GOD?
   You're not going to let them
Get by with it, are you? Not going to walk off
   without *doing* something, are you?

23-26 Please get up—wake up! Tend to my case.
   My God, my Lord—my life is on the line.
Do what you think is right, GOD, my God,
   but don't make me pay for their good time.
Don't let them say to themselves,
   "Ha-ha, we got what we wanted."
Don't let them say,
   "We've chewed him up and spit him out."
Let those who are being hilarious
   at my expense
Be made to look ridiculous.
   Make them wear donkey's ears;
Pin them with the donkey's tail,
   who made themselves so high and mighty!

27-28 But those who want
   the best for me,
Let them have the last word—a glad shout!—
   and say, over and over and over,
"GOD is great—everything works
   together for good for his servant."
I'll tell the world how great and good you are,
   I'll shout Hallelujah all day, every day.

A DAVID PSALM

1-4 **36** The God-rebel tunes in to sedition—
      all ears, eager to sin.
He has no regard for God,
   he stands insolent before him.
He has smooth-talked himself
   into believing
That his evil
   will never be noticed.

Words gutter from his mouth,
   dishwater dirty.
Can't remember when he
   did anything decent.
Every time he goes to bed,
   he fathers another evil plot.
When he's loose on the streets,
   nobody's safe.
He plays with fire
   and doesn't care who gets burned.

God's love is meteoric,   5-6
   his loyalty astronomic,
His purpose titanic,
   his verdicts oceanic.
Yet in his largeness
   nothing gets lost;
Not a man, not a mouse,
   slips through the cracks.

How exquisite your love, O God!   7-9
   How eager we are to run under your wings,
To eat our fill at the banquet you spread
   as you fill our tankards with Eden spring
      water.
You're a fountain of cascading light,
   and you open our eyes to light.

Keep on loving your friends;   10-12
   do your work in welcoming hearts.
Don't let the bullies kick me around,
   the moral midgets slap me down.
Send the upstarts sprawling
   flat on their faces in the mud.

A DAVID PSALM

37 Don't bother your head with braggarts   1-2
   or wish you could succeed like the wicked.
In no time they'll shrivel like grass clippings
   and wilt like cut flowers in the sun.

Get insurance with GOD and do a good deed,   3-4
   settle down and stick to your last.
Keep company with GOD,
   get in on the best.

Open up before GOD, keep nothing back;   5-6
   he'll do whatever needs to be done:
He'll validate your life in the clear light of day
   and stamp you with approval at high noon.

7   Quiet down before God,
       be prayerful before him.
    Don't bother with those who climb the ladder,
       who elbow their way to the top.

8-9 Bridle your anger, trash your wrath,
       cool your pipes—it only makes things worse.
    Before long the crooks will be bankrupt;
       God-investors will soon own the store.

10-11 Before you know it, the wicked will have had it;
       you'll stare at his once famous place and—
          nothing!
    Down-to-earth people will move in and take over,
       relishing a huge bonanza.

12-13 Bad guys have it in for the good guys,
       obsessed with doing them in.
    But God isn't losing any sleep; to him
       they're a joke with no punch line.

14-15 Bullies brandish their swords,
       pull back on their bows with a flourish.
    They're out to beat up on the harmless,
       or mug that nice man out walking his dog.
    A banana peel lands them flat on their faces—
       slapstick figures in a moral circus.

16-17 Less is more and more is less.
       One righteous will outclass fifty wicked,
    For the wicked are moral weaklings
       but the righteous are God-strong.

18-19 God keeps track of the decent folk;
       what they do won't soon be forgotten.
    In hard times, they'll hold their heads high;
       when the shelves are bare, they'll be full.

20   God-despisers have had it;
       God's enemies are finished—
    Stripped bare like vineyards at harvest time,
       vanished like smoke in thin air.

21-22 Wicked borrows and never returns;
       Righteous gives and gives.
    Generous gets it all in the end;
       Stingy is cut off at the pass.

23-24 Stalwart walks in step with God;
       his path blazed by God, he's happy.

If he stumbles, he's not down for long;
    GOD has a grip on his hand.

I once was young, now I'm a graybeard—   25-26
    not once have I seen an abandoned believer,
    or his kids out roaming the streets.
Every day he's out giving and lending,
    his children making him proud.

Turn your back on evil,   27-28
    work for the good and don't quit.
GOD loves this kind of thing,
    never turns away from his friends.

Live this way and you've got it made,   28-29
    but bad eggs will be tossed out.
The good get planted on good land
    and put down healthy roots.

Righteous chews on wisdom like a dog on   30-31
    a bone,
    rolls virtue around on his tongue.
His heart pumps God's Word like blood through
      his veins;
    his feet are as sure as a cat's.

Wicked sets a watch for Righteous,   32-33
    he's out for the kill.
GOD, alert, is also on watch—
    Wicked won't hurt a hair of his head.

Wait passionately for GOD,   34
    don't leave the path.
He'll give you your place in the sun
    while you watch the wicked lose it.

I saw Wicked bloated like a toad,   35-36
    croaking pretentious nonsense.
The next time I looked there was nothing—
    a punctured bladder, vapid and limp.

Keep your eye on the healthy soul,   37-38
    scrutinize the straight life;
There's a future
    in strenuous wholeness.
But the willful will soon be discarded;
    insolent souls are on a dead-end street.

The spacious, free life is from GOD,   39-40
    it's also protected and safe.

GOD-strengthened, we're delivered from evil—
    when we run to him, he saves us.

A DAVID PSALM

38
1-2 Take a deep breath, GOD; calm down—
    don't be so hasty with your punishing rod.
Your sharp-pointed arrows of rebuke draw blood;
    my backside stings from your discipline.

3-4 I've lost twenty pounds in two months
    because of your accusation.
My bones are brittle as dry sticks
    because of my sin.
I'm swamped by my bad behavior,
    collapsed under an avalanche of guilt.

5-8 The cuts in my flesh stink and grow maggots
    because I've lived so badly.
And now I'm flat on my face
    feeling sorry for myself morning to night.
All my insides are on fire,
    my body is a wreck.
I'm on my last legs; I've had it—
    my life is a vomit of groans.

9-16 Lord, my longings are sitting in plain sight,
    my groans an old story to you.
My heart's about to break;
    I'm a burned-out case.
Cataracts blind me to God and good;
    old friends avoid me like the plague.
My cousins never visit,
    my neighbors stab me in the back.
My competitors blacken my name,
    devoutly they pray for my ruin.
But I'm deaf and mute to it all,
    ears shut, mouth shut.
I don't hear a word they say,
    don't speak a word in response.
What I do, GOD, is wait for you,
    wait for my Lord, my God—you *will*
        answer!
I wait and pray so they won't laugh me off,
    won't smugly strut off when I stumble.

17-20 I'm on the edge of losing it—
    the pain in my gut keeps burning.
I'm ready to tell my story of failure,
    I'm no longer smug in my sin.
My enemies are alive and in action,
    a lynch mob after my neck.

I give out good and get back evil
    from God-haters who can't stand a
        God-lover.

Don't dump me, GOD;
    my God, don't stand me up.
Hurry and help me;
    I want some wide-open space in my life!

21-22

A DAVID PSALM
39 I'm determined to watch steps and tongue
    so they won't land me in trouble.
I decided to hold my tongue
    as long as Wicked is in the room.
"Mum's the word," I said, and kept quiet.
    But the longer I kept silence
The worse it got—
    my insides got hotter and hotter.
My thoughts boiled over;
    I spilled my guts.

1-3

"Tell me, what's going on, GOD?
    How long do I have to live?
    Give me the bad news!
You've kept me on pretty short rations;
    my life is a string too short to be saved.
Oh! we're all puffs of air.
    Oh! we're all shadows in a campfire.
Oh! we're just spit in the wind.
    We make our pile, and then we leave it.

4-6

"What am I doing in the meantime, Lord?
    Hoping, that's what I'm doing—hoping
You'll save me from a rebel life,
    save me from the contempt of idiots.
I'll say no more, I'll shut my mouth,
    since you, Lord, are behind all this.
    But I can't take it much longer.
When you put us through the fire
    to purge us from our sin,
    our dearest idols go up in smoke.
Are we also nothing but smoke?

7-11

"Ah, GOD, listen to my prayer, my
    cry—open your ears.
Don't be callous;
    just look at these tears of mine.
I'm a stranger here. I don't know my way—
    a migrant like my whole family.
Give me a break, cut me some slack
    before it's too late and I'm out of here."

12-13

A DAVID PSALM

40

1-3   40 I waited and waited and waited for GOD.
        At last he looked; finally he listened.
He lifted me out of the ditch,
    pulled me from deep mud.
He stood me up on a solid rock
    to make sure I wouldn't slip.
He taught me how to sing the latest God-song,
    a praise-song to our God.
More and more people are seeing this:
    they enter the mystery,
        abandoning themselves to GOD.

4-5   Blessed are you who give yourselves over to GOD,
        turn your backs on the world's "sure thing,"
        ignore what the world worships;
The world's a huge stockpile
    of GOD-wonders and God-thoughts.
Nothing and no one
    compares to you!
I start talking about you, telling what I know,
    and quickly run out of words.
Neither numbers nor words
    account for you.

6   Doing something for you, bringing something
            to you—
        that's not what you're after.
Being religious, acting pious—
    that's not what you're asking for.
You've opened my ears
    so I can listen.

7-8   So I answered, "I'm coming.
        I read in your letter what you wrote about me,
And I'm coming to the party
    you're throwing for me."
That's when God's Word entered my life,
    became part of my very being.

9-10   I've preached you to the whole congregation,
        I've kept back nothing, GOD—you know that.
I didn't keep the news of your ways
    a secret, didn't keep it to myself.
I told it all, how dependable you are, how thorough.
    I didn't hold back pieces of love and truth
For myself alone. I told it all,
    let the congregation know the whole story.

11-12   Now GOD, don't hold out on me,
        don't hold back your passion.

Your love and truth
    are all that keeps me together.
When troubles ganged up on me,
    a mob of sins past counting,
I was so swamped by guilt
    I couldn't see my way clear.
More guilt in my heart than hair on my head,
    so heavy the guilt that my heart gave out.

Soften up, GOD, and intervene;   13-15
    hurry and get me some help,
So those who are trying to kidnap my soul
    will be embarrassed and lose face,
So anyone who gets a kick out of making me miserable
    will be heckled and disgraced,
So those who pray for my ruin
    will be booed and jeered without mercy.

But all who are hunting for you—   16-17
    oh, let them sing and be happy.
Let those who know what you're all about
    tell the world you're great and not quitting.
And me? I'm a mess. I'm nothing and have nothing:
    make something of me.
You can do it; you've got what it takes—
    but God, don't put it off.

A DAVID PSALM

41 Dignify those who are down on their luck;   1-3
    you'll feel good—*that's* what GOD does.
GOD looks after us all,
    makes us robust with life—
Lucky to be in the land,
    we're free from enemy worries.
Whenever we're sick and in bed,
    GOD becomes our nurse,
    nurses us back to health.

I said, "GOD, be gracious!   4-7
    Put me together again—
    my sins have torn me to pieces."
My enemies are wishing the worst for me;
    they make bets on what day I will die.
If someone comes to see me,
    he mouths empty platitudes,
All the while gathering gossip about me
    to entertain the street-corner crowd.
These "friends" who hate me
    whisper slanders all over town.
They form committees
    to plan misery for me.

8-9 The rumor goes out, "He's got some dirty,
    deadly disease. The doctors
    have given up on him."
Even my best friend, the one I always told everything
    —he ate meals at my house all the time!—
    has bitten my hand.

10 GOD, give grace, get me up on my feet.
    I'll show them a thing or two.

11-12 Meanwhile, I'm sure you're on my side—
    no victory shouts yet from the enemy camp!
You know me inside and out, you hold me together,
    you never fail to stand me tall in your presence
    so I can look you in the eye.

13 Blessed is GOD, Israel's God,
    always, always, always.
    Yes. Yes. Yes.

A PSALM OF THE SONS OF KORAH

1-3 **42** A white-tailed deer drinks
      from the creek;
I want to drink God,
    deep drafts of God.
I'm thirsty for God-alive.
I wonder, "Will I ever make it—
    arrive and drink in God's presence?"
I'm on a diet of tears—
    tears for breakfast, tears for supper.
All day long
    people knock at my door,
Pestering,
    "Where is this God of yours?"

4 These are the things I go over and over,
    emptying out the pockets of my life.
I was always at the head of the worshiping crowd,
    right out in front,
Leading them all,
    eager to arrive and worship,
Shouting praises, singing thanksgiving—
    celebrating, all of us, God's feast!

5 Why are you down in the dumps, dear soul?
    Why are you crying the blues?
Fix my eyes on God—
    soon I'll be praising again.
He puts a smile on my face.
    He's my God.

When my soul is in the dumps, I rehearse   6-8
   everything I know of you,
From Jordan depths to Hermon heights,
   including Mount Mizar.
Chaos calls to chaos,
   to the tune of whitewater rapids.
Your breaking surf, your thundering breakers
   crash and crush me.
Then GOD promises to love me all day,
   sing songs all through the night!
   My life is God's prayer.

Sometimes I ask God, my rock-solid God,   9-10
   "Why did you let me down?
Why am I walking around in tears,
   harassed by enemies?"
They're out for the kill, these
   tormentors with their obscenities,
Taunting day after day,
   "Where is this God of yours?"

Why are you down in the dumps, dear soul?   11
   Why are you crying the blues?
Fix my eyes on God—
   soon I'll be praising again.
He puts a smile on my face.
   He's my God.

43 Clear my name, God; stick up for me   1-2
   against these loveless, immoral people.
Get me out of here, away
   from these lying degenerates.
I counted on you, God.
   Why did you walk out on me?
Why am I pacing the floor, wringing my hands
   over these outrageous people?

Give me your lantern and compass,   3-4
   give me a map,
So I can find my way to the sacred mountain,
   to the place of your presence,
To enter the place of worship,
   meet my exuberant God,
Sing my thanks with a harp,
   magnificent God, my God.

Why are you down in the dumps, dear soul?   5
   Why are you crying the blues?
Fix my eyes on God—
   soon I'll be praising again.

FIXING OUR EYES ON GOD

1 What phrases throughout these two psalms are used by the author to describe how they are feeling?

In their original language (Hebrew), these two psalms were typically kept together as one. When we see how they flow together, it's easy to see why. Like a song repeating a chorus, these psalms repeat the same phrase three times. It seems like no matter what happens to this psalmist, they've learned an important lesson: God is bigger than our circumstances. The author makes it clear that they're discouraged but then writes the same chorus again and again (and again) as a reminder of where to focus their attention and find their hope: on God, who "puts a smile on [their] face" (Psalms 42:5, 11; 43:5).

3 What might change in your life if this chorus became your reminder whenever you felt discouraged?

PSALMS 42–43

How do you see the author deal with their pain or stress throughout these psalms?

2

He puts a smile on my face.
　He's my God.

A PSALM OF THE SONS OF KORAH

44 We've been hearing about this, God,
　　all our lives.
Our fathers told us the stories
　their fathers told them,
How single-handedly you weeded out
　　the godless
　from the fields and planted us,
How you sent those people packing
　but gave us a fresh start.
We didn't fight for this land;
　we didn't work for it—it was a gift!
You gave it, smiling as you gave it,
　delighting as you gave it.

1-3

You're my King, O God—
　command victories for Jacob!
With your help we'll wipe out our enemies,
　in your name we'll stomp them to dust.
I don't trust in weapons;
　my sword won't save me—
But it's you, you who saved us from the enemy;
　you made those who hate us lose face.
All day we parade God's praise—
　we thank you by name over and over.

4-8

But now you've walked off and left us,
　you've disgraced us and won't fight for us.
You made us turn tail and run;
　those who hate us have cleaned us out.
You delivered us as sheep to the butcher,
　you scattered us to the four winds.
You sold your people at a discount—
　you made nothing on the sale.

9-12

You made people on the street,
　people we know, poke fun and call us names.
You made us a joke among the godless,
　a cheap joke among the rabble.
Every day I'm up against it,
　my nose rubbed in my shame—
Gossip and ridicule fill the air,
　people out to get me crowd the street.

13-16

All this came down on us,
　and we've done nothing to deserve it.
We never betrayed your Covenant: our hearts
　were never false, our feet never left your path.

17-19

Do we deserve torture in a den of jackals?
    or lockup in a black hole?

20-22   If we had forgotten to pray to our God
    or made fools of ourselves with store-bought gods,
Wouldn't God have figured this out?
    We can't hide things from him.
No, you decided to make us martyrs,
    lambs assigned for sacrifice each day.

23-26   Get up, GOD! Are you going to sleep all day?
    Wake up! Don't you care what happens to us?
Why do you bury your face in the pillow?
    Why pretend things are just fine with us?
And here we are—flat on our faces in the dirt,
    held down with a boot on our necks.
Get up and come to our rescue.
    If you love us so much, *Help us!*

A WEDDING SONG OF THE SONS OF KORAH

1 **45** My heart bursts its banks,
    spilling beauty and goodness.
I pour it out in a poem to the king,
    shaping the river into words:

+   +   +

2-4   "You're the handsomest of men;
    every word from your lips is sheer grace,
    and God has blessed you, blessed you so much.
Strap your sword to your side, warrior!
    Accept praise! Accept due honor!
    Ride majestically! Ride triumphantly!
Ride on the side of truth!
    Ride for the righteous meek!

4-5   "Your instructions are glow-in-the-dark;
    you shoot sharp arrows
Into enemy hearts; the king's
    foes lie down in the dust, beaten.

6-7   "Your throne is God's throne,
    ever and always;
The scepter of your royal rule
    measures right living.
You love the right
    and hate the wrong.
And that is why God, your very own God,
    poured fragrant oil on your head,
Marking you out as king
    from among your dear companions.

"Your forest-drenched garments   8-9
   are fragrant with mountain breeze.
Chamber music—from the throne room—
   makes you want to dance.
Kings' daughters are maids in your court,
   the Bride glittering with golden jewelry.

+   +   +

"Now listen, daughter, don't miss a word: 10-12
   forget your country, put your home behind you.
Be *here*—the king is wild for you.
   Since he's your lord, adore him.
Wedding gifts pour in from Tyre;
   rich guests shower you with presents."

(Her wedding dress is dazzling,   13-15
   lined with gold by the weavers;
All her dresses and robes
   are woven with gold.
She is led to the king,
   followed by her virgin companions.
A procession of joy and laughter!
   a grand entrance to the king's palace!)

"Set your mind now on sons—   16-17
   don't dote on father and grandfather.
You'll set your sons up as princes
   all over the earth.
I'll make you famous for generations;
   you'll be the talk of the town
   for a long, long time."

A SONG OF THE SONS OF KORAH

46 God is a safe place to hide,   1-3
    ready to help when we need him.
We stand fearless at the cliff-edge of doom,
   courageous in seastorm and earthquake,
Before the rush and roar of oceans,
   the tremors that shift mountains.

   Jacob-wrestling God fights for us,
   GOD-of-Angel-Armies protects us.

River fountains splash joy, cooling God's city,   4-6
   this sacred haunt of the Most High.
God lives here, the streets are safe,
   God at your service from crack of dawn.
Godless nations rant and rave, kings and
      kingdoms threaten,
   but Earth does anything he says.

7 Jacob-wrestling God fights for us,
  GOD-of-Angel-Armies protects us.

8-10 Attention, all! See the marvels of GOD!
  He plants flowers and trees all over
      the earth,
  Bans war from pole to pole,
      breaks all the weapons across his knee.
  "Step out of the traffic! Take a long,
      loving look at me, your High God,
      above politics, above everything."

11 Jacob-wrestling God fights for us,
  GOD-of-Angel-Armies protects us.

A PSALM OF THE SONS OF KORAH

1-9 **47** Applause, everyone. Bravo, bravissimo!
      Shout God-songs at the top of your lungs!
  GOD Most High is stunning,
      astride land and ocean.
  He crushes hostile people,
      puts nations at our feet.
  He set us at the head of the line,
      prize-winning Jacob, his favorite.
  Loud cheers as God climbs the mountain,
      a ram's horn blast at the summit.
  Sing songs to God, sing out!
      Sing to our King, sing praise!
  He's Lord over earth,
      so sing your best songs to God.
  God is Lord of godless nations—
      sovereign, he's King of the mountain.
  Princes from all over are gathered,
      people of Abraham's God.
  The powers of earth are God's—
      he soars over all.

A PSALM OF THE SONS OF KORAH

1-3 **48** GOD majestic,
      praise abounds in our God-city!
  His sacred mountain,
      breathtaking in its heights—earth's joy.
  Zion Mountain looms in the North,
      city of the world-King.
  God in his citadel peaks
      undefeatable.

4-6 The kings got together,
      they united and came.
  They took one look and shook their heads,
      they scattered and ran away.

They doubled up in pain
  like a woman having a baby.

You smashed the ships of Tarshish   7-8
  with a storm out of the East.
We heard about it, then we saw it
  with our eyes—
In GOD's city of Angel Armies,
  in the city our God
Set on firm foundations,
  firm forever.

We pondered your love-in-action, God,   9-10
  waiting in your temple:
Your name, God, evokes a train
  of Hallelujahs wherever
It is spoken, near and far;
  your arms are heaped with goodness-in-action.

Be glad, Zion Mountain;   11
  Dance, Judah's daughters!
  He does what he said he'd do!

Circle Zion, take her measure,   12-14
  count her fortress peaks,
Gaze long at her sloping bulwark,
  climb her citadel heights—
Then you can tell the next generation
  detail by detail the story of God,
Our God forever,
  who guides us till the end of time.

A PSALM OF THE SONS OF KORAH

49 Listen, everyone, listen—   1-2
    earth-dwellers, don't miss this.
All you haves
  and have-nots,
All together now: listen.

I set plainspoken wisdom before you,   3-4
  my heart-seasoned understandings of life.
I fine-tuned my ear to the sayings of the wise,
  I solve life's riddle with the help of a harp.

So why should I fear in bad times,   5-6
  hemmed in by enemy malice,
Shoved around by bullies,
  demeaned by the arrogant rich?

Really! There's no such thing as self-rescue,   7-9
  pulling yourself up by your bootstraps.

The cost of rescue is beyond our means,
   and even then it doesn't guarantee
Life forever, or insurance
   against the Black Hole.

10-11   Anyone can see that the brightest and best die,
   wiped out right along with fools and idiots.
They leave all their prowess behind,
   move into their new home, The Coffin,
The cemetery their permanent address.
   And to think they named counties after
      themselves!

12   We aren't immortal. We don't last long.
   Like our dogs, we age and weaken. And die.

13-15   This is what happens to those who live for the moment,
   who only look out for themselves:
Death herds them like sheep straight to hell;
   they disappear down the gullet of the grave;
They waste away to nothing—
   nothing left but a marker in a cemetery.
But me? God snatches me from the clutch of death,
   he reaches down and grabs me.

16-19   So don't be impressed with those who get rich
   and pile up fame and fortune.
They can't take it with them;
   fame and fortune all get left behind.
Just when they think they've arrived
   and folks praise them because they've made good,
They enter the family burial plot
   where they'll never see sunshine again.

20   We aren't immortal. We don't last long.
   Like our dogs, we age and weaken. And die.

AN ASAPH PSALM

1-3   **50** The God of gods—it's GOD!—speaks out, shouts, "Earth!"
      welcomes the sun in the east,
   farewells the disappearing sun in the west.
From the dazzle of Zion,
   God blazes into view.
Our God makes his entrance,
   he's not shy in his coming.
Starbursts of fireworks precede him.

4-5   He summons heaven and earth as a jury,
   he's taking his people to court:
"Round up my saints who swore
   on the Bible their loyalty to me."

NO SUCH THING AS SELF-RESCUE

We live in a culture where independence, wealth, and success are celebrated. But those things don't align with the teachings in this psalm. No one can pull themselves up by their bootstraps—"there's no such thing as self-rescue," this psalmist says (Psalm 49:7). Everyone dies, even the best and brightest. People who "pile up fame and fortune" are just collecting wealth and popularity that will die when they do (Psalm 49:16-19). No matter what we accomplish or earn or achieve, every one of us is still a human being—unable to control the future; incapable of avoiding loss, pain, and death; and just as in need of the love of the God who created us all.

 1
What do you notice about how the rich and successful are described in this psalm?

3 How might you put less effort or worry into your achievements or popularity?

 2
Why do you think the author thinks these are important words to share?

PSALM 49

6 The whole cosmos attests to the fairness of this court,
     that here *God* is judge.

7-15 "Are you listening, dear people? I'm getting ready
         to speak;
       Israel, I'm about ready to bring you to trial.
     This is God, your God,
         speaking to you.
     I don't find fault with your acts of worship,
         the frequent burnt sacrifices you offer.
     But why should I want your blue-ribbon bull,
         or more and more goats from your herds?
     Every creature in the forest is mine,
         the wild animals on all the mountains.
     I know every mountain bird by name;
         the scampering field mice are my friends.
     If I get hungry, do you think I'd tell you?
         All creation and its bounty are mine.
     Do you think I feast on venison?
         or drink drafts of goats' blood?
     Spread for me a banquet of praise,
         serve High God a feast of kept promises,
     And call for help when you're in trouble—
         I'll help you, and you'll honor me."

16-21 Next, God calls up the wicked:

     "What are you up to, quoting my laws,
         talking like we are good friends?
     You never answer the door when I call;
         you treat my words like garbage.
     If you find a thief, you make him your buddy;
         adulterers are your friends of choice.
     Your mouth drools filth;
         lying is a serious art form with you.
     You stab your own brother in the back,
         rip off your little sister.
     I kept a quiet patience while you did these
         things;
         you thought I went along with your game.
     I'm calling you on the carpet, *now*,
         laying your wickedness out in plain sight.

22-23 "Time's up for playing fast and
         loose with me.
     I'm ready to pass sentence,
         and there's no help in sight!
     It's the praising life that honors me.
         As soon as you set your foot on the Way,
     I'll show you my salvation."

**A DAVID PSALM, AFTER HE WAS CONFRONTED BY NATHAN
ABOUT THE AFFAIR WITH BATHSHEBA**

51 Generous in love—God, give grace!   1-3
        Huge in mercy—wipe out my bad record.
Scrub away my guilt,
  soak out my sins in your laundry.
I know how bad I've been;
  my sins are staring me down.

You're the One I've violated, and you've seen   4-6
  it all, seen the full extent of my evil.
You have all the facts before you;
  whatever you decide about me is fair.
I've been out of step with you for a long time,
  in the wrong since before I was born.
What you're after is truth from the inside out.
  Enter me, then; conceive a new, true life.

Soak me in your laundry and I'll come out clean,   7-15
  scrub me and I'll have a snow-white life.
Tune me in to foot-tapping songs,
  set these once-broken bones to dancing.
Don't look too close for blemishes,
  give me a clean bill of health.
God, make a fresh start in me,
  shape a Genesis week from the chaos of my life.
Don't throw me out with the trash,
  or fail to breathe holiness in me.
Bring me back from gray exile,
  put a fresh wind in my sails!
Give me a job teaching rebels your ways
  so the lost can find their way home.
Commute my death sentence, God, my
    salvation God,
  and I'll sing anthems to your life-giving ways.
Unbutton my lips, dear God;
  I'll let loose with your praise.

Going through the motions doesn't please you,   16-17
  a flawless performance is nothing to you.
I learned God-worship
  when my pride was shattered.
Heart-shattered lives ready for love
  don't for a moment escape God's notice.

Make Zion the place you delight in,   18-19
  repair Jerusalem's broken-down walls.
Then you'll get real worship from us,
  acts of worship small and large,
Including all the bulls
  they can heave onto your altar!

**A DAVID PSALM, WHEN DOEG THE EDOMITE REPORTED TO SAUL,
"DAVID'S AT AHIMELECH'S HOUSE"**

1-4 **52** Why do you brag of evil, "Big Man"?
God's mercy carries the day.
You scheme catastrophe;
your tongue cuts razor-sharp,
artisan in lies.
You love evil more than good,
you call black white.
You love malicious gossip,
you foul-mouth.

5 God will tear you limb from limb,
sweep you up and throw you out,
Pull you up by the roots
from the land of life.

6-7 Good people will watch and
worship. They'll laugh in relief:
"Big Man bet on the wrong horse,
trusted in big money,
made his living from catastrophe."

8 And I'm an olive tree,
growing green in God's house.
I trusted in the generous mercy
of God then and now.

9 I thank you always
that you went into action.
And I'll stay right here,
your good name my hope,
in company with your faithful friends.

A DAVID PSALM

1-2 **53** Bilious and bloated, they gas,
"God is gone."
It's poison gas—
they foul themselves, they poison
Rivers and skies;
thistles are their cash crop.
God sticks his head out of heaven.
He looks around.
He's looking for someone not stupid—
one man, even, God-expectant,
just one God-ready woman.

3 He comes up empty. A string
of zeros. Useless, unshepherded
Sheep, taking turns pretending
to be Shepherd.

The ninety and nine
    follow the one.

Don't they know anything,   4
    all these predators?
Don't they know
    they can't get away with this,
Treating people like a fast-food meal
    over which they're too busy to pray?

Night is coming for them, and nightmare—   5
    a nightmare they'll never wake up from.
God will make hash of these squatters,
    send them packing for good.

Is there anyone around to save Israel?   6
    God turns life around.
Turned-around Jacob skips rope,
    turned-around Israel sings laughter.

A DAVID PSALM, WHEN THE ZIPHITES REPORTED TO SAUL, "DAVID IS HIDING OUT WITH US"
54 God, for your sake, help me!   1-2
    Use your influence to clear me.
Listen, God—I'm desperate.
    Don't be too busy to hear me.

Outlaws are out to get me,   3
    hit men are trying to kill me.
Nothing will stop them;
    God means nothing to them.

Oh, look! God's right here helping!   4-5
    GOD's on my side,
Evil is looping back on my enemies.
    Don't let up! Finish them off!

I'm ready now to worship, so ready.   6-7
    I thank you, GOD—you're so good.
You got me out of every scrape,
    and I saw my enemies get it.

A DAVID PSALM
55 Open your ears, God, to my prayer;   1-3
    don't pretend you don't hear me knocking.
Come close and whisper your answer.
    I really need you.
I shudder at the mean voice,
    quail before the evil eye,
As they pile on the guilt,
    stockpile angry slander.

4-8 My insides are turned inside out;
    specters of death have me down.
I shake with fear,
    I shudder from head to foot.
"Who will give me wings," I ask—
    "wings like a dove?"
Get me out of here on dove wings;
    I want some peace and quiet.
I want a walk in the country,
    I want a cabin in the woods.
I'm desperate for a change
    from rage and stormy weather.

9-11 Come down hard, Lord—slit their tongues.
    I'm appalled how they've split the city
Into rival gangs
    prowling the alleys
Day and night spoiling for a fight,
    trash piled in the streets,
Even shopkeepers gouging and cheating
    in broad daylight.

12-14 This isn't the neighborhood bully
    mocking me—I could take that.
This isn't a foreign devil spitting
    invective—I could tune that out.
It's *you*! We grew up together!
    You! My best friend!
Those long hours of leisure as we walked
    arm in arm, God a third party to our
        conversation.

15 Haul my betrayers off alive to hell—let them
    experience the horror, let them
    feel every desolate detail of a damned life.

16-19 I call to God;
    GOD will help me.
At dusk, dawn, and noon I sigh
    deep sighs—he hears, he rescues.
My life is well and whole, secure
    in the middle of danger
Even while thousands
    are lined up against me.
God hears it all, and from his judge's bench
    puts them in their place.
But, set in their ways, they won't change;
    they pay him no mind.

20-21 And this, my best friend, betrayed his best friends;
    his life betrayed his word.

All my life I've been charmed by his speech,
    never dreaming he'd turn on me.
His words, which were music to my ears,
    turned to daggers in my heart.

Pile your troubles on GOD's shoulders—   22-23
    he'll carry your load, he'll help you out.
He'll never let good people
    topple into ruin.
But you, God, will throw the others
    into a muddy bog,
Cut the lifespan of assassins
    and traitors in half.

And I trust in you.

A DAVID PSALM, WHEN HE WAS CAPTURED BY THE PHILISTINES IN GATH

56 Take my side, God—I'm getting kicked around,   1-4
    stomped on every day.
Not a day goes by
    but somebody beats me up;
They make it their duty
    to beat me up.
When I get really afraid
    I come to you in trust.
I'm proud to praise God;
    fearless now, I trust in God.
    What can mere mortals do?

They don't let up—   5-6
    they smear my reputation
    and huddle to plot my collapse.
They gang up,
    sneak together through the alleys
To take me by surprise,
    wait their chance to get me.

Pay them back in evil!   7
    Get angry, God!
    Down with these people!

You've kept track of my every toss   8
    and turn
    through the sleepless nights,
Each tear entered in your ledger,
    each ache written in your book.

If my enemies run away,   9
    turn tail when I yell at them,
Then I'll know
    that God is on my side.

10-11 I'm proud to praise God,
proud to praise GOD.
Fearless now, I trust in God;
what can mere mortals do to me?

12-13 God, you did everything you promised,
and I'm thanking you with all my heart.
You pulled me from the brink of death,
my feet from the cliff-edge of doom.
Now I stroll at leisure with God
in the sunlit fields of life.

A DAVID PSALM, WHEN HE HID IN A CAVE FROM SAUL

1-3 **57** Be good to me, God—and now!
I've run to you for dear life.
I'm hiding out under your wings
until the hurricane blows over.
I call out to High God,
the God who holds me together.
He sends orders from heaven and saves me,
he humiliates those who kick me around.
God delivers generous love,
he makes good on his word.

4 I find myself in a pride of lions
who are wild for a taste of human flesh;
Their teeth are lances and arrows,
their tongues are sharp daggers.

5 Soar high in the skies, O God!
Cover the whole earth with your glory!

6 They booby-trapped my path;
I thought I was dead and done for.
They dug a mantrap to catch me,
and fell in headlong themselves.

7-8 I'm ready, God, so ready,
ready from head to toe,
Ready to sing, ready to raise a tune:
"Wake up, soul!
Wake up, harp! wake up, lute!
Wake up, you sleepyhead sun!"

9-10 I'm thanking you, GOD, out loud in the streets,
singing your praises in town and country.
The deeper your love, the higher it goes;
every cloud is a flag to your faithfulness.

11 Soar high in the skies, O God!
Cover the whole earth with your glory!

A DAVID PSALM

58 Is this any way to run a country? 1-2
Is there an honest politician in the house?
Behind the scenes you weave webs of deceit,
behind closed doors you make deals with demons.

The wicked crawl from the wrong side of the cradle; 3-5
their first words out of the womb are lies.
Poison, lethal rattlesnake poison,
drips from their forked tongues—
Deaf to threats, deaf to charm,
decades of wax built up in their ears.

God, smash their teeth to bits, 6-9
leave them toothless tigers.
Let their lives be buckets of water spilled,
all that's left, a damp stain in the sand.
Let them be trampled grass
worn smooth by the traffic.
Let them dissolve into snail slime,
be a miscarried fetus that never sees sunlight.
Before what they cook up is half-done, God,
throw it out with the garbage!

The righteous will call up their friends 10-11
when they see the wicked get their reward,
Serve up their blood in goblets
as they toast one another,
Everyone cheering, "It's worth it to play by the rules!
God's handing out trophies and tending the earth!"

**A DAVID PSALM, WHEN SAUL SET A WATCH ON DAVID'S HOUSE
IN ORDER TO KILL HIM**

59 My God! Rescue me from my enemies, 1-2
defend me from these mutineers.
Rescue me from their dirty tricks,
save me from their hit men.

Desperadoes have ganged up on me, 3-4
they're hiding in ambush for me.
I did nothing to deserve this, GOD,
crossed no one, wronged no one.
All the same, they're after me,
determined to get me.

Wake up and see for yourself! You're GOD, 4-5
GOD-of-Angel-Armies, Israel's God!
Get on the job and take care of these pagans,
don't be soft on these hard cases.

They return when the sun goes down, 6-7
They howl like coyotes, ringing the city.

Then suddenly they're all at the gate,
    Snarling invective, drawn daggers in their teeth.
    They think they'll never get caught.

8-10 But you, GOD, break out laughing;
    you treat the godless nations like jokes.
Strong God, I'm watching you do it,
    I can always count on you.
God in dependable love shows up on time,
    shows me my enemies in ruin.

11-13 Don't make quick work of them, GOD,
    lest my people forget.
Bring them down in slow motion,
    take them apart piece by piece.
Let all their mean-mouthed arrogance
    catch up with them,
Catch them out and bring them down
    —every muttered curse
    —every barefaced lie.
Finish them off in fine style!
    Finish them off for good!
Then all the world will see
    that God rules well in Jacob,
    everywhere that God's in charge.

14-15 They return when the sun goes down,
    They howl like coyotes, ringing the city.
They scavenge for bones,
    And bite the hand that feeds them.

16-17 And me? I'm singing your prowess,
    shouting at dawn your largesse,
For you've been a safe place for me,
    a good place to hide.
Strong God, I'm watching you do it,
    I can always count on you—
    God, my dependable love.

**A DAVID PSALM, WHEN HE FOUGHT AGAINST ARAM-NAHARAIM AND ARAM-ZOBAH
AND JOAB KILLED TWELVE THOUSAND EDOMITES AT THE VALLEY OF SALT**

1-2 **60** God! you walked off and left us,
    kicked our defenses to bits
And stomped off angry.
    Come back. Oh please, come back!

You shook earth to the foundations,
    ripped open huge crevasses.
Heal the breaks! Everything's
    coming apart at the seams.

You made your people look doom in the face,   3-5
   then gave us cheap wine to drown our troubles.
Then you planted a flag to rally your people,
   an unfurled flag to look to for courage.
Now do something quickly, answer right now,
   so the one you love best is saved.

That's when God spoke in holy splendor,   6-8
   "Bursting with joy,
I make a present of Shechem,
   I hand out Succoth Valley as a gift.
Gilead's in my pocket,
   to say nothing of Manasseh.
Ephraim's my hard hat,
   Judah my hammer;
Moab's a scrub bucket,
   I mop the floor with Moab,
Spit on Edom,
   rain fireworks all over Philistia."

Who will take me to the thick of the fight?   9-10
   Who'll show me the road to Edom?
You aren't giving up on us, are you, God?
   refusing to go out with our troops?

Give us help for the hard task;   11-12
   human help is worthless.
In God we'll do our very best;
   he'll flatten the opposition for good.

A DAVID PSALM

61   God, listen to me shout,   1-2
     bend an ear to my prayer.
When I'm far from anywhere,
   down to my last gasp,
I call out, "Guide me
   up High Rock Mountain!"

You've always given me breathing room,   3-5
   a place to get away from it all,
A lifetime pass to your safe-house,
   an open invitation as your guest.
You've always taken me seriously, God,
   made me welcome among those who know and
      love you.

Let the days of the king add up   6-8
   to years and years of good rule.
Set his throne in the full light of God;
   post Steady Love and Good Faith as lookouts,

And I'll be the poet who sings your glory—
    and live what I sing every day.

A DAVID PSALM

1-2 **62** God, the one and only—
      I'll wait as long as he says.
Everything I need comes from him,
    so why not?
He's solid rock under my feet,
    breathing room for my soul,
An impregnable castle:
    I'm set for life.

3-4 How long will you gang up on me?
    How long will you run with the bullies?
There's nothing to you, any of you—
    rotten floorboards, worm-eaten rafters,
Anthills plotting to bring down mountains,
    far gone in make-believe.
You talk a good line,
    but every "blessing" breathes a curse.

5-6 God, the one and only—
    I'll wait as long as he says.
Everything I hope for comes from him,
    so why not?
He's solid rock under my feet,
    breathing room for my soul,
An impregnable castle:
    I'm set for life.

7-8 My help and glory are in God
    —granite-strength and safe-harbor-God—
So trust him absolutely, people;
    lay your lives on the line for him.
    God is a safe place to be.

9 Man as such is smoke,
    woman as such, a mirage.
Put them together, they're nothing;
    two times nothing is nothing.

10 And a windfall, if it comes—
    don't make too much of it.

11 God said this once and for all;
    how many times
Have I heard it repeated?
    "Strength comes
Straight from God."

There are words in this passage that feel pretty harsh: "Man . . . is smoke, woman . . . a mirage. Put them together, they're nothing" (Psalm 62:9). Even with their efforts combined, humans can do essentially . . . zero? We know that's not literally true, but the author is setting up a comparison. It's true that humans are capable of a lot. What's also true, though, is that compared to the wisdom, power, and love of God, human abilities and impact do look pretty small. This doesn't mean that we should give up on ourselves but rather that we have a home in something much, much bigger: "God is a safe place to be," this psalmist writes (Psalm 62:8).

Why do you think the author repeats that God is "the one and only" (Psalm 62:1, 5)?
2

3 Is there something you're trying to take control of that you should trust God with instead?

1 What do you notice about the way God is described in this passage?

PSALM 62

TWO TIMES NOTHING IS NOTHING

12 Love to you, Lord God!
You pay a fair wage for a good day's work!

A DAVID PSALM, WHEN HE WAS OUT IN THE JUDEAN WILDERNESS

1 **63** God—you're my God!
I can't get enough of you!
I've worked up such hunger and thirst for God,
traveling across dry and weary deserts.

2-4 So here I am in the place of worship, eyes open,
drinking in your strength and glory.
In your generous love I am really living at last!
My lips brim praises like fountains.
I bless you every time I take a breath;
My arms wave like banners of praise to you.

5-8 I eat my fill of prime rib and gravy;
I smack my lips. It's time to shout praises!
If I'm sleepless at midnight,
I spend the hours in grateful reflection.
Because you've always stood up for me,
I'm free to run and play.
I hold on to you for dear life,
and you hold me steady as a post.

9-11 Those who are out to get me are marked for doom,
marked for death, bound for hell.
They'll die violent deaths;
jackals will tear them limb from limb.
But the king is glad in God;
his true friends spread the joy,
While small-minded gossips
are gagged for good.

A DAVID PSALM

1 **64** Listen and help, O God.
I'm reduced to a whine
And a whimper, obsessed
with feelings of doomsday.

2-6 Don't let them find me—
the conspirators out to get me,
Using their tongues as weapons,
flinging poison words,
poison-tipped arrow-words.
They shoot from ambush,
shoot without warning,
not caring who they hit.
They keep fit doing calisthenics
of evil purpose,

They keep lists of the traps
    they've secretly set.
They say to each other,
    "No one can catch us,
    no one can detect our perfect crime."
The Detective detects the mystery
    in the dark of the cellar heart.

The God of the Arrow shoots!   7-8
    They double up in pain,
Fall flat on their faces
    in full view of the grinning crowd.

Everyone sees it. God's   9-10
    work is the talk of the town.
Be glad, good people! Fly to GOD!
    Good-hearted people, make praise your habit.

A DAVID PSALM

65 Silence is praise to you,   1-2
    Zion-dwelling God,
And also obedience.
    You hear the prayer in it all.

We all arrive at your doorstep sooner   2-8
    or later, loaded with guilt,
Our sins too much for us—
    but you get rid of them once and for all.
Blessed are the chosen! Blessed the guest
    at home in your place!
We expect our fill of good things
    in your house, your heavenly manse.
All your salvation wonders
    are on display in your trophy room.
Earth-Tamer, Ocean-Pourer,
    Mountain-Maker, Hill-Dresser,
Muzzler of sea storm and wave crash,
    of mobs in noisy riot—
Far and wide they'll come to a stop,
    they'll stare in awe, in wonder.
Dawn and dusk take turns
    calling, "Come and worship."

Oh, visit the earth,   9-13
    ask her to join the dance!
Deck her out in spring showers,
    fill the God-River with living water.
Paint the wheat fields golden.
    Creation was made for this!
Drench the plowed fields,
    soak the dirt clods

With rainfall as harrow and rake
    bring her to blossom and fruit.
Snow-crown the peaks with splendor,
    scatter rose petals down your paths,
All through the wild meadows, rose petals.
    Set the hills to dancing,
Dress the canyon walls with live sheep,
    a drape of flax across the valleys.
Let them shout, and shout, and shout!
    Oh, oh, let them sing!

1-4 **66** All together now—applause for God!
    Sing songs to the tune of his glory,
    set glory to the rhythms of his praise.
Say of God, "We've never seen anything like him!"
    When your enemies see you in action,
    they slink off like scolded dogs.
The whole earth falls to its knees—
    it worships you, sings to you,
    can't stop enjoying your name and fame.

5-6 Take a good look at God's wonders—
    they'll take your breath away.
He converted sea to dry land;
    travelers crossed the river on foot.
    Now isn't that cause for a song?

7 Ever sovereign in his high tower, he keeps
    his eye on the godless nations.
Rebels don't dare
    raise a finger against him.

8-12 Bless our God, O peoples!
    Give him a thunderous welcome!
Didn't he set us on the road to life?
    Didn't he keep us out of the ditch?
He trained us first,
    passed us like silver through refining fires,
Brought us into hardscrabble country,
    pushed us to our very limit,
Road-tested us inside and out,
    took us to hell and back;
Finally he brought us
    to this well-watered place.

13-15 I'm bringing my prizes and presents to your house.
    I'm doing what I said I'd do,
What I solemnly swore I'd do
    that day when I was in so much trouble:
The choicest cuts of meat
    for the sacrificial meal;

Even the fragrance
  of roasted lamb is like a meal!
Or make it an ox
  garnished with goat meat!

All believers, come here and listen,   16-20
  let me tell you what God did for me.
I called out to him with my mouth,
  my tongue shaped the sounds of music.
If I had been cozy with evil,
  the Lord would never have listened.
But he most surely *did* listen,
  he came on the double when he heard
      my prayer.
Blessed be God: he didn't turn a deaf ear,
  he stayed with me, loyal in his love.

67 God, mark us with grace   1-7
   and blessing! Smile!
The whole country will see how you work,
  all the godless nations see how you save.
God! Let people thank and enjoy you.
  Let all people thank and enjoy you.
Let all far-flung people become happy
  and shout their happiness because
You judge them fair and square,
  you tend the far-flung peoples.
God! Let people thank and enjoy you.
  Let all people thank and enjoy you.
Earth, display your exuberance!
  You mark us with blessing, O God,
      our God.
You mark us with blessing, O God.
  Earth's four corners—honor him!

A DAVID PSALM
68 Up with God!   1-4
   Down with his enemies!
  Adversaries, run for the hills!
Gone like a puff of smoke,
  like a blob of wax in the fire—
      one look at God and the wicked vanish.
When the righteous see God in action
  they'll laugh, they'll sing,
      they'll laugh and sing for joy.
Sing hymns to God;
  all heaven, sing out;
      clear the way for the coming of Cloud-Rider.
Enjoy GOD,
  cheer when you see him!

5-6   Father of orphans,
      champion of widows,
         is God in his holy house.
    God makes homes for the homeless,
      leads prisoners to freedom,
         but leaves rebels to rot in hell.

7-10   God, when you took the lead with your people,
      when you marched out into the wild,
    Earth shook, sky broke out in a sweat;
      God was on the march.
    Even Sinai trembled at the sight of God on
      the move,
      at the sight of Israel's God.
    You pour out rain in buckets, O God;
      thorn and cactus become an oasis
    For your people to camp in and enjoy.
      You set them up in business;
      they went from rags to riches.

11-14   The Lord gave the word;
      thousands called out the good news:
    "Kings of the armies
      are on the run, on the run!"
    While housewives, safe and sound back home,
      divide up the plunder,
      the plunder of Canaanite silver and gold.
    On that day that Shaddai scattered the kings,
      snow fell on Black Mountain.

15-16   You huge mountains, Bashan mountains,
      mighty mountains, dragon mountains.
    All you mountains not chosen,
      sulk now, and feel sorry for yourselves,
    For this is the mountain God has chosen to live on;
      he'll rule from this mountain forever.

17-18   The chariots of God, twice ten thousand,
      and thousands more besides,
    The Lord in the lead, riding down Sinai—
      straight to the Holy Place!
    You climbed to the High Place, captives in tow,
      your arms full of plunder from rebels,
    And now you sit there in state,
      GOD, sovereign GOD!

19-23   Blessed be the Lord—
      day after day he carries us along.
    He's our Savior, our God, oh yes!
      He's God-for-us, he's God-who-saves-us.

Lord GOD knows all
   death's ins and outs.
What's more, he made heads roll,
   split the skulls of the enemy
As he marched out of heaven,
    saying, "I tied up the Dragon in knots,
    put a muzzle on the Deep Blue Sea."
You can wade through your enemies' blood,
    and your dogs taste of your enemies from
       your boots.

See God on parade 24-31
   to the sanctuary, my God,
   my King on the march!
Singers out front, the band behind,
   maidens in the middle with castanets.
The whole choir blesses God.
    Like a fountain of praise, Israel blesses GOD.
Look—little Benjamin's out
   front and leading
Princes of Judah in their royal robes,
   princes of Zebulun, princes of Naphtali.
Parade your power, O God,
   the power, O God, that made us what we are.
Your temple, High God, is Jerusalem;
   kings bring gifts to you.
Rebuke that old crocodile, Egypt,
   with her herd of wild bulls and calves,
Rapacious in her lust for silver,
   crushing peoples, spoiling for a fight.
Let Egyptian traders bring blue cloth
   and Cush come running to God, her hands
      outstretched.

Sing, O kings of the earth! 32-34
   Sing praises to the Lord!
There he is: Sky-Rider,
   striding the ancient skies.
Listen—he's calling in thunder,
   rumbling, rolling thunder.
Call out "Bravo!" to God,
   the High God of Israel.
His splendor and strength
   rise huge as thunderheads.

A terrible beauty, O God, 35
   streams from your sanctuary.
It's Israel's strong God! He gives
   power and might to his people!
O you, his people—bless God!

A DAVID PSALM

1 **69** God, God, save me!
I'm in over my head,

2 Quicksand under me, swamp water over me;
I'm going down for the third time.

3 I'm hoarse from calling for help,
Bleary-eyed from searching the sky for God.

4 I've got more enemies than hairs on my head;
Liars and cheats are out to knife me in
        the back.

What I never stole
Must I now give back?

5 God, you know every sin I've committed;
My life's a wide-open book before you.

6 Don't let those who look to you in hope
Be discouraged by what happens to me,
Dear Lord! GOD of the armies!

Don't let those out looking for you
Come to a dead end by following me—
Please, dear God of Israel!

7 Because of you I look like an idiot,
I walk around ashamed to show my face.

8 My brothers shun me like a bum off the street;
My family treats me like an unwanted guest.

9 I love you more than I can say.
Because I'm madly in love with you,
They blame me for everything they dislike
        about you.

10 When I poured myself out in prayer and fasting,
All it got me was more contempt.

11 When I put on a sad face,
They treated me like a clown.

12 Now drunks and gluttons
Make up drinking songs about me.

13 And me? I pray.
GOD, it's time for a break!

God, answer in love!
Answer with your sure salvation!

Rescue me from the swamp, 14
Don't let me go under for good,

Pull me out of the clutch of the enemy;
This whirlpool is sucking me down.

Don't let the swamp be my grave, the Black Hole 15
Swallow me, its jaws clenched around me.

Now answer me, GOD, because you love me; 16
Let me see your great mercy full-face.

Don't look the other way; your servant can't take it. 17
I'm in trouble. Answer right now!

Come close, God; get me out of here. 18
Rescue me from this deathtrap.

You know how they kick me around— 19
Pin on me the donkey's ears, the dunce's cap.

I'm broken by their taunts, 20
Flat on my face, reduced to a nothing.

I looked in vain for one friendly face. Not one.
I couldn't find one shoulder to cry on.

They put poison in my soup, 21
Vinegar in my drink.

Let their supper be bait in a trap that snaps shut; 22
May their best friends be trappers who'll skin them alive.

Make them become blind as bats, 23
Give them the shakes from morning to night.

Let them know what you think of them, 24
Blast them with your red-hot anger.

Burn down their houses, 25
Leave them desolate with nobody at home.

They gossiped about the one you disciplined, 26
Made up stories about anyone wounded by God.

Pile on the guilt, 27
Don't let them off the hook.

28 Strike their names from the list of the living;
No rock-carved honor for them among the
righteous.

29 I'm hurt and in pain;
Give me space for healing, and mountain air.

30 Let me shout God's name with a praising song,
Let me tell his greatness in a prayer of thanks.

31 For GOD, this is better than oxen on the altar,
Far better than blue-ribbon bulls.

32 The poor in spirit see and are glad—
Oh, you God-seekers, take heart!

33 For GOD listens to the poor,
He doesn't walk out on the wretched.

34 You heavens, praise him; praise him, earth;
Also ocean and all things that swim in it.

35 For God is out to help Zion,
Rebuilding the wrecked towns of Judah.

Guess who will live there—
The proud owners of the land?

36 No, the children of his servants will get it,
The lovers of his name will live in it.

A DAVID PRAYER

1-3 **70** God! Please hurry to my rescue!
GOD, come quickly to my side!
Those who are out to get me—
let them fall all over themselves.
Those who relish my downfall—
send them down a blind alley.
Give them a taste of their own medicine,
those gossips off clucking their tongues.

4 Let those on the hunt for you
sing and celebrate.
Let all who love your saving way
say over and over, "God is mighty!"

5 But I've lost it. I'm wasted.
God—quickly, quickly!
Quick to my side, quick to my rescue!
GOD, don't lose a minute.

71

I run for dear life to GOD,
   I'll never live to regret it.
Do what you do so well:
   get me out of this mess and up on my feet.
Put your ear to the ground and listen,
   give me space for salvation.
Be a guest room where I can retreat;
   you said your door was always open!
You're my salvation—my vast, granite fortress.

My God, free me from the grip of Wicked,
   from the clutch of Bad and Bully.
You keep me going when times are tough—
   my bedrock, GOD, since my childhood.
I've hung on you from the day of my birth,
   the day you took me from the cradle;
   I'll never run out of praise.
Many gasp in alarm when they see me,
   but you take me in stride.

Just as each day brims with your beauty,
   my mouth brims with praise.
But don't turn me out to pasture when I'm old
   or put me on the shelf when I can't pull my weight.
My enemies are talking behind my back,
   watching for their chance to knife me.
The gossip is: "God has abandoned him.
   Pounce on him now; no one will help him."

God, don't just watch from the sidelines.
   Come on! Run to my side!
My accusers—make them lose face.
   Those out to get me—make them look
Like idiots, while I stretch out, reaching for you,
   and daily add praise to praise.
I'll write the book on your righteousness,
   talk up your salvation all the day long,
   never run out of good things to write or say.
I come in the power of the Lord GOD,
   I post signs marking his right-of-way.

You got me when I was an unformed youth,
   God, and taught me everything I know.
Now I'm telling the world your wonders;
   I'll keep at it until I'm old and gray.
God, don't walk off and leave me
   until I get out the news
Of your strong right arm to this world,
   news of your power to the world yet to come,
Your famous and righteous
   ways, O God.

We can easily get caught up in the current moment and forget that our actions today will have an impact on our future. But this psalm reminds us that God will be with us even when times are tough, even when we're eventually old and gray. As we seek to grow in our faith and become who God created us to be, we can take comfort in knowing that God's love for us will never fade. Let's make the most of every opportunity we have to serve God and keep "telling the world [God's] wonders" until we're "old and gray" (Psalm 71:17-18).

How can you make the most of your opportunities to serve God in your current season of life?

3

2 How does this psalm challenge your perspective about the future and the impact of your present actions?

1

How does this psalmist describe the faithful love of God throughout every season of life?

PSALM 71

TILL I'M OLD AND GRAY

God, you've done it all!
    Who is quite like you?
You, who made me stare trouble in the face,
    Turn me around;
Now let me look life in the face.
    I've been to the bottom;
Bring me up, streaming with honors;
    turn to me, be tender to me,
And I'll take up the lute and thank you
    to the tune of your faithfulness, God.
I'll make music for you on a harp,
    Holy One of Israel.
When I open up in song to you,
    I let out lungsful of praise,
        my rescued life a song.
All day long I'm chanting
    about you and your righteous ways,
While those who tried to do me in
    slink off looking ashamed.

A SOLOMON PSALM

72 Give the gift of wise rule to the king, O God,   1-8
        the gift of just rule to the crown prince.
May he judge your people rightly,
    be honorable to your meek and lowly.
Let the mountains give exuberant witness;
    shape the hills with the contours of right living.
Please stand up for the poor,
    help the children of the needy,
        come down hard on the cruel tyrants.
Outlast the sun, outlive the moon—
    age after age after age.
Be rainfall on cut grass,
    earth-refreshing rain showers.
Let righteousness burst into blossom
    and peace abound until the moon fades
        to nothing.
Rule from sea to sea,
    from the River to the Rim.

Foes will fall on their knees before God,   9-14
    his enemies lick the dust.
Kings remote and legendary will pay homage,
    kings rich and resplendent will turn over their
        wealth.
All kings will fall down and worship,
    and godless nations sign up to serve him,
Because he rescues the poor at the first sign of need,
    the destitute who have run out of luck.
He opens a place in his heart for the down-and-out,
    he restores the wretched of the earth.

He frees them from tyranny and torture—
    when they bleed, he bleeds;
    when they die, he dies.

15-17 And live! Oh, let him live!
    Deck him out in Sheba gold.
Offer prayers unceasing to him,
    bless him from morning to night.
Fields of golden grain in the land,
    cresting the mountains in wild exuberance,
Cornucopias of praise, praises
    springing from the city like grass from
        the earth.
May he never be forgotten,
    his fame shine on like sunshine.
May all godless people enter his circle of blessing
    and bless the One who blessed them.

18-20 Blessed GOD, Israel's God,
    the one and only wonder-working God!
Blessed always his blazing glory!
    All earth brims with his glory.
Yes and Yes and Yes.

AN ASAPH PSALM

1-5 **73** No doubt about it! God is good—
    good to good people, good to the good-hearted.
But I nearly missed it,
    missed seeing his goodness.
I was looking the other way,
    looking up to the people
At the top,
    envying the wicked who have it made,
Who have nothing to worry about,
    not a care in the whole wide world.

6-10 Pretentious with arrogance,
    they wear the latest fashions in violence,
Pampered and overfed,
    decked out in silk bows of silliness.
They jeer, using words to kill;
    they bully their way with words.
They're full of hot air,
    loudmouths disturbing the peace.
People actually listen to them—can you believe it?
    Like thirsty puppies, they lap up their words.

11-14 What's going on here? Is God out to lunch?
    Nobody's tending the store.
The wicked get by with everything;
    they have it made, piling up riches.

I've been stupid to play by the rules;
　　what has it gotten me?
A long run of bad luck, that's what—
　　a slap in the face every time I walk out the door.

If I'd have given in and talked like this,　　15-20
　　I would have betrayed your dear children.
Still, when I tried to figure it out,
　　all I got was a splitting headache . . .
Until I entered the sanctuary of God.
　　Then I saw the whole picture:
The slippery road you've put them on,
　　with a final crash in a ditch of delusions.
In the blink of an eye, disaster!
　　A blind curve in the dark, and—nightmare!
We wake up and rub our eyes. . . . Nothing.
　　There's nothing to them. And there never was.

When I was beleaguered and bitter,　　21-24
　　totally consumed by envy,
I was totally ignorant, a dumb ox
　　in your very presence.
I'm still in your presence,
　　but you've taken my hand.
You wisely and tenderly lead me,
　　and then you bless me.

You're all I want in heaven!　　25-28
　　You're all I want on earth!
When my skin sags and my bones get brittle,
　　GOD is rock-firm and faithful.
Look! Those who left you are falling apart!
　　Deserters, they'll never be heard from again.
But I'm in the very presence of God—
　　oh, how refreshing it is!
I've made Lord GOD my home.
　　God, I'm telling the world what you do!

AN ASAPH PSALM

74 You walked off and left us, and never looked back.　　1
　　God, how could you do that?
We're your very own sheep;
　　how can you stomp off in anger?

Refresh your memory of us—you bought us a long　　2-3
　　　time ago.
　　Your most precious tribe—you paid a good price for us!
　　Your very own Mount Zion—you actually lived
　　　here once!
Come and visit the site of disaster,
　　see how they've wrecked the sanctuary.

4-8 While your people were at worship, your enemies barged in,
　　　brawling and scrawling graffiti.
They set fire to the porch;
　　　axes swinging, they chopped up the woodwork,
Beat down the doors with sledgehammers,
　　　then split them into kindling.
They burned your holy place to the ground,
　　　violated the place of worship.
They said to themselves, "We'll wipe them all out,"
　　　and burned down all the places of worship.

9-17 There's not a sign or symbol of God in sight,
　　　nor anyone to speak in his name,
　　　no one who knows what's going on.
How long, God, will barbarians blaspheme,
　　　enemies curse and get by with it?
Why don't you do something? How long are you going
　　　to sit there with your hands folded in your lap?
God is my King from the very start;
　　　he works salvation in the womb of the earth.
With one blow you split the sea in two,
　　　you made mincemeat of the dragon Tannin.
You lopped off the heads of Leviathan,
　　　then served them up in a stew for the animals.
With your finger you opened up springs and creeks,
　　　and dried up the wild floodwaters.
You own the day, you own the night;
　　　you put stars and sun in place.
You laid out the four corners of earth,
　　　shaped the seasons of summer and winter.

18-21 Mark and remember, GOD, all the enemy
　　　taunts, each idiot desecration.
Don't throw your lambs to the wolves;
　　　after all we've been through, don't forget us.
Remember your promises;
　　　the city is in darkness, the countryside violent.
Don't leave the victims to rot in the street;
　　　make them a choir that sings your praises.

22-23 On your feet, O God—
　　　stand up for yourself!
Do you hear what they're saying about you,
　　　all the vile obscenities?
Don't tune out their malicious filth,
　　　the brawling invective that never lets up.

AN ASAPH PSALM

1　**75** We thank you, God, we thank you—
　　　your Name is our favorite word;
　　　your mighty works are all we talk about.

You say, "I'm calling this meeting to order,   2-4
   I'm ready to set things right.
When the earth goes topsy-turvy
   And nobody knows which end is up,
I nail it all down,
   I put everything in place again.
I say to the smart alecks, 'That's enough,'
   to the bullies, 'Not so fast.'"

Don't raise your fist against High God.   5-6
   Don't raise your voice against Rock of Ages.
He's the One from east to west;
   from desert to mountains, he's the One.

God rules: he brings this one down to his knees,   7-8
   pulls that one up on her feet.
GOD has a cup in his hand,
   a bowl of wine, full to the brim.
He draws from it and pours;
   it's drained to the dregs.
Earth's wicked ones drink it all,
   drink it down to the last bitter drop!

And I'm telling the story of God Eternal,   9-10
   singing the praises of Jacob's God.
The fists of the wicked
   are bloody stumps,
The arms of the righteous
   are lofty green branches.

AN ASAPH PSALM

76 God is well-known in Judah;   1-3
   in Israel, he's a household name.
He keeps a house in Salem,
   his own suite of rooms in Zion.
That's where, using arrows for kindling,
   he made a bonfire of weapons of war.

Oh, how bright you shine!   4-6
   Outshining their huge piles of loot!
The warriors were plundered
   and left there impotent.
And now there's nothing to them,
   nothing to show for their swagger and threats.
Your sudden roar, God of Jacob,
   knocked the wind out of horse and rider.

Fierce you are, and fearsome!   7-10
   Who can stand up to your rising anger?
From heaven you thunder judgment;
   earth falls to her knees and holds her breath.

God stands tall and makes things right,
    he saves all the wretched on earth.
Instead of smoldering rage—God-praise!
    All that sputtering rage—now a garland for God!

11-12   Do for GOD what you said you'd do—
    he is, after all, your God.
Let everyone in town bring offerings
    to the One Who Watches our every move.
Nobody gets by with anything,
    no one plays fast and loose with him.

AN ASAPH PSALM

77   I yell out to my God, I yell with all my might,
    I yell at the top of my lungs. He listens.

2-6   I found myself in trouble and went looking for my Lord;
    my life was an open wound that wouldn't heal.
When friends said, "Everything will turn out all right,"
    I didn't believe a word they said.
I remember God—and shake my head.
    I bow my head—then wring my hands.
I'm awake all night—not a wink of sleep;
    I can't even say what's bothering me.
I go over the days one by one,
    I ponder the years gone by.
I strum my lute all through the night,
    wondering how to get my life together.

7-10   Will the Lord walk off and leave us for good?
    Will he never smile again?
Is his love worn threadbare?
    Has his salvation promise burned out?
Has God forgotten his manners?
    Has he angrily stomped off and left us?
"Just my luck," I said. "The High God retires
    just the moment I need him."

11-12   Once again I'll go over what GOD has done,
    lay out on the table the ancient wonders;
I'll ponder all the things you've accomplished,
    and give a long, loving look at your acts.

13-15   O God! Your way is holy!
    No god is great like God!
You're the God who makes things happen;
    you showed everyone what you can do—
You pulled your people out of the worst kind
      of trouble,
    rescued the children of Jacob and Joseph.

FREE TO YELL

② Why is it important that the psalmist expresses these feelings, even when they're complicated?

PSALM 77

What do you notice about the tone at the beginning of this psalm versus the tone at the end?

①

These words are raw and honest. This psalmist is yelling at God, in trouble, desperate, and hurting. This person's life is "an open wound" (Psalm 77:2)—a deep pain that just won't heal. And even though they believe in God, even though it becomes clear later in the psalm how deeply they trust God, they feel distrustful at the same time: "Will the Lord walk off and leave us for good? . . . Is his love worn threadbare?" (Psalm 77:7-8). Trust and distrust often live side by side within us, and this psalm emphasizes how normal and okay it is to express that reality—especially to God.

③ Can you think of a time when you've both trusted and distrusted God or another person?

16-19 Ocean saw you in action, God,
saw you and trembled with fear;
Deep Ocean was scared to death.
Clouds belched buckets of rain,
Sky exploded with thunder,
your arrows flashing this way and that.
From Whirlwind came your thundering voice,
Lightning exposed the world,
Earth reeled and rocked.
You strode right through Ocean,
walked straight through roaring Ocean,
but nobody saw you come or go.

20 Hidden in the hands of Moses and Aaron,
You led your people like a flock of sheep.

AN ASAPH PSALM

1-4 **78** Listen, dear friends, to God's truth,
bend your ears to what I tell you.
I'm chewing on the morsel of a proverb;
I'll let you in on the sweet old truths,
Stories we heard from our fathers,
counsel we learned at our mother's knee.
We're not keeping this to ourselves,
we're passing it along to the next
generation—
GOD's fame and fortune,
the marvelous things he has done.

5-8 He planted a witness in Jacob,
set his Word firmly in Israel,
Then commanded our parents
to teach it to their children
So the next generation would know,
and all the generations to come—
Know the truth and tell the stories
so their children can trust in God,
Never forget the works of God
but keep his commands to the letter.
Heaven forbid they should be like their parents,
bullheaded and bad,
A fickle and faithless bunch
who never stayed true to God.

9-16 The Ephraimites, armed to the teeth,
ran off when the battle began.
They were cowards to God's Covenant,
refused to walk by his Word.
They forgot what he had done—
marvels he'd done right before their eyes.

He performed miracles in plain sight of their parents
   in Egypt, out on the fields of Zoan.
He split the Sea and they walked right through it;
   he piled the waters to the right and the left.
He led them by day with a cloud,
   led them all the night long with a fiery torch.
He split rocks in the wilderness,
   gave them all they could drink from underground springs;
He made creeks flow out from sheer rock,
   and water pour out like a river.

All they did was sin even more,   17-20
   rebel in the desert against the High God.
They tried to get their own way with God,
   clamored for favors, for special attention.
They whined like spoiled children,
   "Why can't God give us a decent meal in this desert?"
Sure, he struck the rock and the water flowed,
   creeks cascaded from the rock.
But how about some fresh-baked bread?
   How about a nice cut of meat?"

When GOD heard that, he was furious—   21-31
   his anger flared against Jacob,
   he lost his temper with Israel.
It was clear they didn't believe God,
   had no intention of trusting in his help.
But God helped them anyway, commanded the clouds
   and gave orders that opened the gates of heaven.
He rained down showers of manna to eat,
   he gave them the Bread of Heaven.
They ate the bread of the mighty angels;
   he sent them all the food they could eat.
He let East Wind break loose from the skies,
   gave a strong push to South Wind.
This time it was birds that rained down—
   succulent birds, an abundance of birds.
He aimed them right for the center of their camp;
   all round their tents there were birds.
They ate and had their fill;
   he handed them everything they craved on a platter.
But their greed knew no bounds;
   they stuffed their mouths with more and more.
Finally, God was fed up, his anger erupted—
   he cut down their brightest and best,
   he laid low Israel's finest young men.

And—can you believe it?—they kept right on sinning;   32-37
   all those wonders and they still wouldn't believe!
So their lives wasted away to nothing—
   nothing to show for their lives but a ghost town.

When he cut them down, they came running
    for help;
  they turned and pled for mercy.
They gave witness that God was their rock,
    that High God was their redeemer,
But they didn't mean a word of it;
    they lied through their teeth the whole time.
They could not have cared less about him,
    wanted nothing to do with his Covenant.

38-55 And God? Compassionate!
    Forgave the sin! Didn't destroy!
Over and over he reined in his anger,
    restrained his considerable wrath.
He knew what they were made of;
    he knew there wasn't much to them,
How often in the desert they had spurned him,
    tried his patience in those wilderness years.
Time and again they pushed him to the limit,
    provoked Israel's Holy God.
How quickly they forgot what he'd done,
    forgot their day of rescue from the enemy,
When he did miracles in Egypt,
    wonders on the plain of Zoan.
He turned the River and its streams to blood—
    not a drop of water fit to drink.
He sent flies, which ate them alive,
    and frogs, which drove them crazy.
He turned their harvest over to caterpillars,
    everything they had worked for to the locusts.
He flattened their grapevines with hail;
    a killing frost ruined their orchards.
He pounded their cattle with hail,
    let thunderbolts loose on their herds.
His anger flared,
    a wild firestorm of havoc,
An advance guard of disease-carrying angels
    to clear the ground, preparing the way before him.
He didn't spare those people,
    he let the plague rage through their lives.
He killed all the Egyptian firstborns,
    lusty infants, offspring of Ham's virility.
Then he led his people out like sheep,
    took his flock safely through the wilderness.
He took good care of them; they had nothing to fear.
    The Sea took care of their enemies for good.
He brought them into his holy land,
    this mountain he claimed for his own.
He scattered everyone who got in their way;
    he staked out an inheritance for them—
    the tribes of Israel all had their own places.

But they kept on giving him a hard time,
    rebelled against God, the High God,
    refused to do anything he told them.
They were worse, if that's possible, than their parents:
    traitors—crooked as a corkscrew.
Their pagan orgies provoked God's anger,
    their obscene idolatries broke his heart.
When God heard their carryings-on, he was furious;
    he posted a huge No over Israel.
He walked off and left Shiloh empty,
    abandoned the shrine where he had met with Israel.
He let his pride and joy go to the dogs,
    turned his back on the pride of his life.
He turned them loose on fields of battle;
    angry, he let them fend for themselves.
Their young men went to war and never came back;
    their young women waited in vain.
Their priests were massacred,
    and their widows never shed a tear.

Suddenly the Lord was up on his feet
    like someone roused from deep sleep,
    shouting like a drunken warrior.
He hit his enemies hard, sent them running,
    yelping, not daring to look back.
He disqualified Joseph as leader,
    told Ephraim he didn't have what it takes,
And chose the Tribe of Judah instead,
    Mount Zion, which he loves so much.
He built his sanctuary there, resplendent,
    solid and lasting as the earth itself.
Then he chose David, his servant,
    handpicked him from his work in the sheep pens.
One day he was caring for the ewes and their lambs,
    the next day God had him shepherding Jacob,
    his people Israel, his prize possession.
His good heart made him a good shepherd;
    he guided the people wisely and well.

AN ASAPH PSALM

79 God! Barbarians have broken into your home,
    violated your holy temple,
    left Jerusalem a pile of rubble!
They've served up the corpses of your servants
    as carrion food for birds of prey,
Threw the bones of your holy people
    out to the wild animals to gnaw on.
They dumped out their blood
    like buckets of water.
All around Jerusalem, their bodies
    were left to rot, unburied.

56-64

65-72

1-4

We're nothing but a joke to our neighbors,
    graffiti scrawled on the city walls.

5-7 How long do we have to put up with this, GOD?
    Do you have it in for us for good?
    Will your smoldering rage never cool down?
If you're going to be angry, be angry
    with the pagans who care nothing about you,
    or your rival kingdoms who ignore you.
They're the ones who ruined Jacob,
    who wrecked and looted the place where he lived.

8-10 Don't blame us for the sins of our parents.
    Hurry up and help us; we're at the end of our rope.
You're famous for helping; God, give *us* a break.
    Your reputation is on the line.
Pull us out of this mess, forgive us our sins—
    do what you're famous for doing!
Don't let the heathen get by with their sneers:
    "Where's your God? Is he out to lunch?"
Go public and show the godless world
    that they can't kill your servants and get by with it.

11-13 Give groaning prisoners a hearing;
    pardon those on death row from their doom—you can do it!
Give our jeering neighbors what they've got coming to them;
    let their God-taunts boomerang and knock them flat.
Then we, your people, the ones you love and care for,
    will thank you over and over and over.
We'll tell everyone we meet
    how wonderful you are, how praiseworthy you are!

AN ASAPH PSALM

1-2 **80** Listen, Shepherd, Israel's Shepherd—
    get all your Joseph sheep together.
Throw beams of light
    from your dazzling throne
So Ephraim, Benjamin, and Manasseh
    can see where they're going.
Get out of bed—you've slept long enough!
    Come on the run before it's too late.

3 God, come back!
    Smile your blessing smile:
    That will be our salvation.

4-6 GOD, God-of-the-Angel-Armies,
    how long will you smolder like a sleeping volcano
    while your people call for fire and brimstone?
You put us on a diet of tears,
    bucket after bucket of salty tears to drink.

You make us look ridiculous to our friends;
    our enemies poke fun day after day.

God-of-the-Angel-Armies, come back!   7
Smile your blessing smile:
That will be our salvation.

Remember how you brought a young vine from Egypt,   8-18
    cleared out the brambles and briers
    and planted your very own vineyard?
You prepared the good earth,
    you planted her roots deep;
    the vineyard filled the land.
Your vine soared high and shaded the mountains,
    even dwarfing the giant cedars.
Your vine ranged west to the Sea,
    east to the River.
So why do you no longer protect your vine?
    Trespassers pick its grapes at will;
Wild pigs crash through and crush it,
    and the mice nibble away at what's left.
God-of-the-Angel-Armies, turn our way!
    Take a good look at what's happened
    and attend to this vine.
Care for what you once tenderly planted—
    the vine you raised from a shoot.
And those who dared to set it on fire—
    give them a look that will kill!
Then take the hand of your once-favorite child,
    the child you raised to adulthood.
We will never turn our back on you;
    breathe life into our lungs so we can shout your name!

GOD, God-of-the-Angel-Armies, come back!   19
Smile your blessing smile:
That will be our salvation.

AN ASAPH PSALM

81
A song to our strong God!   1-5
    a shout to the God of Jacob!
Anthems from the choir, music from the band,
    sweet sounds from lute and harp,
Trumpets and trombones and horns:
    it's festival day, a feast to God!
A day decreed by God,
    solemnly ordered by the God of Jacob.
He commanded Joseph to keep this day
    so we'd never forget what he did in Egypt.

I hear this most gentle whisper from One
I never guessed would speak to me:

6-7 "I took the world off your shoulders,
  freed you from a life of hard labor.
You called to me in your pain;
  I got you out of a bad place.
I answered you from where the thunder hides,
  I proved you at Meribah Fountain.

8-10 "Listen, dear ones—get this straight;
  O Israel, don't take this lightly.
Don't take up with strange gods,
  don't worship the popular gods.
I'm GOD, your God, the very God
  who rescued you from doom in Egypt,
Then fed you all you could eat,
  filled your hungry stomachs.

11-12 "But my people didn't listen,
  Israel paid no attention;
So I let go of the reins and told them, 'Run!
  Do it your own way!'

13-16 "Oh, dear people, will you listen to
    me now?
  Israel, will you follow my map?
I'll make short work of your enemies,
  give your foes the back of my hand.
I'll send the GOD-haters cringing like dogs,
  never to be heard from again.
You'll feast on my fresh-baked bread
  spread with butter and rock-pure honey."

AN ASAPH PSALM

1 **82** God calls the judges into his courtroom,
  he puts all the judges in the dock.

2-4 "Enough! You've corrupted justice long enough,
  you've let the wicked get away with murder.
You're here to defend the defenseless,
  to make sure that underdogs get a fair break;
Your job is to stand up for the powerless,
  and prosecute all those who exploit them."

5 Ignorant judges! Head-in-the-sand judges!
  They haven't a clue to what's going on.
And now everything's falling apart,
  the world's coming unglued.

6-7 "I appointed you judges, each one of you,
  deputies of the High God,
But you've betrayed your commission
  and now you're stripped of your rank, busted."

O God, give them what they've got coming!   8
    You've got the whole world in your hands!

AN ASAPH PSALM

83 GOD, don't shut me out;   1-5
    don't give me the silent treatment, O God.
Your enemies are out there whooping it up,
    the God-haters are living it up;
They're plotting to do your people in,
    conspiring to rob you of your precious ones.
"Let's wipe this nation from the face of the earth,"
    they say; "scratch Israel's name off the books."
And now they're putting their heads together,
    making plans to get rid of you.

    Edom and the Ishmaelites,   6-8
    Moab and the Hagrites,
    Gebal and Ammon and Amalek,
    Philistia and the Tyrians,
    And now Assyria has joined up,
    Giving muscle to the gang of Lot.

Do to them what you did to Midian,   9-12
    to Sisera and Jabin at Kishon Brook;
They came to a bad end at Endor,
    nothing but dung for the garden.
Cut down their leaders as you did Oreb and Zeeb,
    their princes to nothings like Zebah and Zalmunna,
With their empty brags, "We're grabbing it all,
    grabbing God's gardens for ourselves."

My God! I've had it with them!   13-18
    Blow them away!
Tumbleweeds in the desert waste,
    charred sticks in the burned-over ground.
Knock the breath right out of them, so they're gasping
    for breath, gasping, "GOD."
Bring them to the end of their rope,
    and leave them there dangling, helpless.
Then they'll learn your name: "GOD,"
    the one and only High God on earth.

A KORAH PSALM

84 What a beautiful home, GOD-of-the-Angel-Armies!   1-2
    I've always longed to live in a place like this,
Always dreamed of a room in your house,
    where I could sing for joy to God-alive!

Birds find nooks and crannies in your house,   3-4
    sparrows and swallows make nests there.

They lay their eggs and raise their young,
    singing their songs in the place where we worship.
God-of-the-Angel-Armies! King! God!
    How blessed they are to live and sing there!

5-7 And how blessed all those in whom you live,
    whose lives become roads you travel;
They wind through lonesome valleys, come upon brooks,
    discover cool springs and pools brimming with rain!
God-traveled, these roads curve up the mountain, and
    at the last turn—Zion! God in full view!

8-9 God-of-the-Angel-Armies, listen:
    O God of Jacob, open your ears—I'm praying!
Look at our shields, glistening in the sun,
    our faces, shining with your gracious anointing.

10-12 One day spent in your house, this beautiful place
      of worship,
    beats thousands spent on Greek island beaches.
I'd rather scrub floors in the house of my God
    than be honored as a guest in the palace of sin.
All sunshine and sovereign is God,
    generous in gifts and glory.
He doesn't scrimp with his traveling companions.
    It's smooth sailing all the way with God-of-the-Angel-Armies.

A KORAH PSALM

1-3 **85** God, you smiled on your good earth!
    You brought good times back to Jacob!
You lifted the cloud of guilt from your people,
    you put their sins far out of sight.
You took back your sin-provoked threats,
    you cooled your hot, righteous anger.

4-7 Help us again, God of our help;
    don't hold a grudge against us forever.
You aren't going to keep this up, are you?
    scowling and angry, year after year?
Why not help us make a fresh start—a resurrection life?
    Then your people will laugh and sing!
Show us how much you love us, God!
    Give us the salvation we need!

8-9 I can't wait to hear what he'll say.
    God's about to pronounce his people well,
The holy people he loves so much,
    so they'll never again live like fools.
See how close his salvation is to those who fear him?
    Our country is home base for Glory!

Love and Truth meet in the street,
 Right Living and Whole Living embrace and kiss!   10-13
Truth sprouts green from the ground,
 Right Living pours down from the skies!
Oh yes! GOD gives Goodness and Beauty;
 our land responds with Bounty and Blessing.
Right Living strides out before him,
 and clears a path for his passage.

A DAVID PSALM

86 Bend an ear, GOD; answer me.   1-7
 I'm one miserable wretch!
Keep me safe—haven't I lived a good life?
 Help your servant—I'm depending on you!
You're my God; have mercy on me.
 I count on you from morning to night.
Give your servant a happy life;
 I put myself in your hands!
You're well-known as good and forgiving,
 bighearted to all who ask for help.
Pay attention, GOD, to my prayer;
 bend down and listen to my cry for help.
Every time I'm in trouble I call on you,
 confident that you'll answer.

There's no one quite like you among the gods, O Lord,   8-10
 and nothing to compare with your works.
All the nations you made are on their way,
 ready to give honor to you, O Lord,
Ready to put your beauty on display,
 parading your greatness,
And the great things you do—
 God, you're the one, there's no one but you!

Train me, GOD, to walk straight;   11-17
 then I'll follow your true path.
Put me together, one heart and mind;
 then, undivided, I'll worship in joyful fear.
From the bottom of my heart I thank you, dear Lord;
 I've never kept secret what you're up to.
You've always been great toward me—what love!
 You snatched me from the brink of disaster!
God, these bullies have reared their heads!
 A gang of thugs is after me—
 and they don't care a thing about you.
But you, O God, are both tender and kind,
 not easily angered, immense in love,
 and you never, never quit.
So look me in the eye and show kindness,
 give your servant the strength to go on,
 save your dear, dear child!

GOD NEVER, NEVER QUITS

3 How easy or difficult
is it for you to share
your real thoughts,
feelings, and fears
with God?

Having a long, ongoing, everyday conversation with God is a really beautiful thing. The Psalms express the vast range of feelings, fears, difficulties with faith, and insecurities that so many of us experience. And yet we can see here that, despite many major struggles, this psalmist knows that God has never ceased to show love, forgiveness, patience, and mercy. "You, O God, are both tender and kind, not easily angered, immense in love, and you never, never quit," they write (Psalm 86:15). The author believes that no matter what feeling or fear or doubt they express, God's love and grace will never change. All of it is welcome.

PSALM 86

How does
the psalmist
show that they
depend on God?
1

2 What kinds
of things does
the author ask for
God's help with?

Make a show of how much you love me
  so the bullies who hate me will stand there
      slack-jawed,
As you, GOD, gently and powerfully
  put me back on my feet.

A KORAH PSALM

87 He founded Zion on the Holy Mountain—   1-3
        and oh, how GOD loves his home!
Loves it far better than all
  the homes of Jacob put together!
God's hometown—oh!
  everyone there is talking about you!

I name them off, those among whom I'm famous: 4
  Egypt and Babylon,
  also Philistia,
  even Tyre, along with Cush.
Word's getting around; they point them out:
  "This one was born again here!"

The word's getting out on Zion: 5
  "Men and women, right and left,
  get born again in her!"

GOD registers their names in his book: 6
  "This one, this one, and this one—
  born again, right here."

Singers and dancers give credit to Zion: 7
  "All my springs are in you!"

A KORAH PRAYER OF HEMAN

88 GOD, you're my last chance of the day.   1-9
        I spend the night on my knees before you.
Put me on your salvation agenda;
  take notes on the trouble I'm in.
I've had my fill of trouble;
  I'm camped on the edge of hell.
I'm written off as a lost cause,
  one more statistic, a hopeless case.
Abandoned as already dead,
  one more body in a stack of corpses,
And not so much as a gravestone—
  I'm a black hole in oblivion.
You've dropped me into a bottomless pit,
  sunk me in a pitch-black abyss.
I'm battered senseless by your rage,
  relentlessly pounded by your waves of anger.
You turned my friends against me,
  made me horrible to them.

I'm caught in a maze and can't find my way out,
    blinded by tears of pain and frustration.

9-12   I call to you, GOD; all day I call.
    I wring my hands, I plead for help.
Are the dead a live audience for your miracles?
    Do ghosts ever join the choirs that praise you?
Does your love make any difference in a graveyard?
    Is your faithful presence noticed in the corridors of hell?
Are your marvelous wonders ever seen in the dark,
    your righteous ways noticed in the Land of No Memory?

13-18   I'm standing my ground, GOD, shouting for help,
    at my prayers every morning, on my knees each daybreak.
Why, GOD, do you turn a deaf ear?
    Why do you make yourself scarce?
For as long as I remember I've been hurting;
    I've taken the worst you can hand out, and I've had it.
Your wildfire anger has blazed through my life;
    I'm bleeding, black-and-blue.
You've attacked me fiercely from every side,
    raining down blows till I'm nearly dead.
You made lover and neighbor alike dump me;
    the only friend I have left is Darkness.

AN ETHAN PRAYER

1-4 **89** Your love, GOD, is my song, and I'll sing it!
    I'm forever telling everyone how faithful you are.
I'll never quit telling the story of your love—
    how you built the cosmos
    and guaranteed everything in it.
Your love has always been our lives' foundation,
    your fidelity has been the roof over our world.
You once said, "I joined forces with my chosen leader,
    I pledged my word to my servant, David, saying,
'Everyone descending from you is guaranteed life;
    I'll make your rule as solid and lasting as rock.'"

5-18   GOD! Let the cosmos praise your wonderful ways,
    the choir of holy angels sing anthems to your faithful ways!
Search high and low, scan skies and land,
    you'll find nothing and no one quite like GOD.
The holy angels are in awe before him;
    he looms immense and august over everyone
        around him.
GOD-of-the-Angel-Armies, who is like you,
    powerful and faithful from every angle?
You put the arrogant ocean in its place
    and calm its waves when they turn unruly.
You gave that old hag Egypt the back of your hand,
    you brushed off your enemies with a flick of your wrist.

You own the cosmos—you made everything in it,
  everything from atom to archangel.
You positioned the North and South Poles;
  the mountains Tabor and Hermon sing duets to you.
With your well-muscled arm and your grip of steel—
  nobody messes with you!
The Right and Justice are the roots of your rule;
  Love and Truth are its fruits.
Blessed are the people who know the passwords of praise,
  who shout on parade in the bright presence of GOD.
Delighted, they dance all day long; they know
  who you are, what you do—they can't keep it quiet!
Your vibrant beauty has gotten inside us—
  you've been so good to us! We're walking on air!
All we are and have we owe to GOD,
  Holy God of Israel, our King!

A long time ago you spoke in a vision,   19-37
  you spoke to your faithful beloved:
"I've crowned a hero,
  I chose the best I could find;
I found David, my servant,
  poured holy oil on his head,
And I'll keep my hand steadily on him,
  yes, I'll stick with him through thick and thin.
No enemy will get the best of him,
  no scoundrel will do him in.
I'll weed out all who oppose him,
  I'll clean out all who hate him.
I'm with him for good and I'll love him forever;
  I've set him on high—he's riding high!
I've put Ocean in his one hand, River in the other;
  he'll call out, 'Oh, my Father—my God, my Rock of Salvation!'
Yes, I'm setting him apart as the First of the royal line,
  High King over all of earth's kings.
I'll preserve him eternally in my love,
  I'll faithfully do all I so solemnly promised.
I'll guarantee his family tree
  and underwrite his rule.
If his children refuse to do what I tell them,
  if they refuse to walk in the way I show them,
If they spit on the directions I give them
  and tear up the rules I post for them—
I'll rub their faces in the dirt of their rebellion
  and make them face the music.
But I'll never throw them out,
  never abandon or disown them.
Do you think I'd withdraw my holy promise?
  or take back words I'd already spoken?
I've given my word, my whole and holy word;
  do you think I would lie to David?

His family tree is here for good,
   his sovereignty as sure as the sun,
Dependable as the phases of the moon,
   inescapable as weather."

³⁸⁻⁵² But GOD, you did walk off and leave us,
   you lost your temper with the one you anointed.
You tore up the promise you made to your servant,
   you stomped his crown in the mud.
You blasted his home to kingdom come,
   reduced his city to a pile of rubble
Picked clean by wayfaring strangers,
   a joke to all the neighbors.
You declared a holiday for all his enemies,
   and they're celebrating for all they're worth.
Angry, you opposed him in battle,
   refused to fight on his side;
You robbed him of his splendor, humiliated this warrior,
   ground his kingly honor in the dirt.
You took the best years of his life
   and left him an impotent, ruined husk.
How long do we put up with this, GOD?
   Are you gone for good? Will you hold this grudge forever?
Remember my sorrow and how short life is.
   Did you create men and women for nothing but this?
We'll see death soon enough. Everyone does.
   And there's no back door out of hell.
So where is the love you're so famous for, Lord?
   What happened to your promise to David?
Take a good look at your servant, dear Lord;
   I'm the butt of the jokes of all nations,
The taunting jokes of your enemies, GOD,
   as they dog the steps of your dear anointed.

        Blessed be GOD forever and always!
            Yes. Oh, yes.

A PRAYER OF MOSES, MAN OF GOD

¹⁻² **90** God, it seems you've been our home forever;
            long before the mountains were born,
Long before you brought earth itself to birth,
   from "once upon a time" to "kingdom come"—you are God.

³⁻¹¹ So don't return us to mud, saying,
      "Back to where you came from!"
Patience! You've got all the time in the world—whether
   a thousand years or a day, it's all the same to you.
Are we no more to you than a wispy dream,
   no more than a blade of grass
That springs up gloriously with the rising sun
   and is cut down without a second thought?

Your anger is far and away too much for us;
    we're at the end of our rope.
You keep track of all our sins; every misdeed
    since we were children is entered in your books.
All we can remember is that frown on your face.
    Is that all we're ever going to get?
We live for seventy years or so
    (with luck we might make it to eighty),
And what do we have to show for it? Trouble.
    Toil and trouble and a marker in the graveyard.
Who can make sense of such rage,
    such anger against the very ones who fear you?

Oh! Teach us to live well!   12-17
    Teach us to live wisely and well!
Come back, GOD—how long do we have to wait?—
    and treat your servants with kindness for a change.
Surprise us with love at daybreak;
    then we'll skip and dance all the day long.
Make up for the bad times with some good times;
    we've seen enough evil to last a lifetime.
Let your servants see what you're best at—
    the ways you rule and bless your children.
And let the loveliness of our Lord, our God, rest on us,
    confirming the work that we do.
    Oh, yes. Affirm the work that we do!

91 You who sit down in the High God's presence,   1-13
    spend the night in Shaddai's shadow,
Say this: "GOD, you're my refuge.
    I trust in you and I'm safe!"
That's right—he rescues you from hidden traps,
    shields you from deadly hazards.
His huge outstretched arms protect you—
    under them you're perfectly safe;
    his arms fend off all harm.
Fear nothing—not wild wolves in the night,
    not flying arrows in the day,
Not disease that prowls through the darkness,
    not disaster that erupts at high noon.
Even though others succumb all around,
    drop like flies right and left,
    no harm will even graze you.
You'll stand untouched, watch it all from a distance,
    watch the wicked turn into corpses.
Yes, because GOD's your refuge,
    the High God your very own home,
Evil can't get close to you,
    harm can't get through the door.
He ordered his angels
    to guard you wherever you go.

If you stumble, they'll catch you;
    their job is to keep you from falling.
You'll walk unharmed among lions and snakes,
    and kick young lions and serpents from the path.

14-16 "If you'll hold on to me for dear life," says GOD,
    "I'll get you out of any trouble.
I'll give you the best of care
    if you'll only get to know and trust me.
Call me and I'll answer, be at your side in bad times;
    I'll rescue you, then throw you a party.
I'll give you a long life,
    give you a long drink of salvation!"

A SABBATH SONG

1-3 **92** What a beautiful thing, GOD, to give thanks,
    to sing an anthem to you, the High God!
To announce your love each daybreak,
    sing your faithful presence all through the night,
Accompanied by dulcimer and harp,
    the full-bodied music of strings.

4-9 You made me so happy, GOD.
    I saw your work and I shouted for joy.
How magnificent your work, GOD!
    How profound your thoughts!
Dullards never notice what you do;
    fools never do get it.
When the wicked popped up like weeds
    and all the evil men and women took over,
You mowed them down,
    finished them off once and for all.
You, GOD, are High and Eternal.
    Look at your enemies, GOD!
Look at your enemies—ruined!
    Scattered to the winds, all those hirelings of evil!

10-14 But you've made me strong as a charging bison,
    you've honored me with a festive parade.
The sight of my critics going down is still fresh,
    the rout of my malicious detractors.
My ears are filled with the sounds of promise:
    "Good people will prosper like palm trees,
Grow tall like Lebanon cedars;
    transplanted to GOD's courtyard,
They'll grow tall in the presence of God,
    lithe and green, virile still in old age."

15 Such witnesses to upright GOD!
    My Mountain, my huge, holy Mountain!

93 God is King, robed and ruling,
God is robed and surging with strength.

And yes, the world is firm, immovable,
Your throne ever firm—you're Eternal!

Sea storms are up, God,
Sea storms wild and roaring,
Sea storms with thunderous breakers.

Stronger than wild sea storms,
Mightier than sea-storm breakers,
Mighty God rules from High Heaven.

What you say goes—it always has.
"Beauty" and "Holy" mark your palace rule,
God, to the very end of time.

94 God, put an end to evil;
avenging God, show your colors!
Judge of the earth, take your stand;
throw the book at the arrogant.

God, the wicked get away with murder—
how long will you let this go on?
They brag and boast
and crow about their crimes!

They walk all over your people, God,
exploit and abuse your precious people.
They take out anyone who gets in their way;
if they can't use them, they kill them.
They think, "God isn't looking,
Jacob's God is out to lunch."

Well, think again, you idiots,
fools—how long before you get smart?
Do you think Ear-Maker doesn't hear,
Eye-Shaper doesn't see?
Do you think the trainer of nations doesn't
correct,
the teacher of Adam doesn't know?
God knows, all right—
knows your stupidity,
sees your shallowness.

How blessed the man you train, God,
the woman you instruct in your Word,
Providing a circle of quiet within the clamor of evil,
while a jail is being built for the wicked.

GOD will never walk away from his people,
    never desert his precious people.
Rest assured that justice is on its way
    and every good heart put right.

16-19   Who stood up for me against the wicked?
    Who took my side against evil workers?
If GOD hadn't been there for me,
    I never would have made it.
The minute I said, "I'm slipping, I'm falling,"
    your love, GOD, took hold and held me fast.
When I was upset and beside myself,
    you calmed me down and cheered me up.

20-23   Can Misrule have anything in common with you?
    Can Troublemaker pretend to be on your side?
They ganged up on good people,
    plotted behind the backs of the innocent.
But GOD became my hideout,
    God was my high mountain retreat,
Then boomeranged their evil back on them:
    for their evil ways he wiped them out,
    our GOD cleaned them out for good.

1-2 **95** Come, let's shout praises to GOD,
    raise the roof for the Rock who saved us!
Let's march into his presence singing praises,
    lifting the rafters with our hymns!

3-5   And why? Because GOD is the best,
    High King over all the gods.
In one hand he holds deep caves and caverns,
    in the other hand grasps the high mountains.
He made Ocean—he owns it!
    His hands sculpted Earth!

6-7   So come, let us worship: bow before him,
    on your knees before GOD, who made us!
Oh yes, he's our God,
    and we're the people he pastures, the flock he feeds.

7-11   Drop everything and listen, listen as he speaks:
    "Don't turn a deaf ear as in the Bitter Uprising,
As on the day of the Wilderness Test,
    when your ancestors turned and put *me* to the test.
For forty years they watched me at work among them,
    as over and over they tried my patience.
And I was provoked—oh, was I provoked!
    'Can't they keep their minds on God for five minutes?
    Do they simply refuse to walk down my road?'

You, like all people, probably have times when you feel anxious, uncertain, or even unimportant. This psalm reminds us of the power and majesty of God, the creator of everything. It's pretty wild—the all-powerful being who "made Ocean" and "sculpted Earth" also made us! This God is *our* God, and *we're* the people God pastures (Psalm 95:5-7). No matter how uncertain or lonely we feel or how challenging our lives may get, God is always there to guide us. How can we not say, "GOD is the best" (Psalm 95:3)? We can be filled with hope, strength, and confidence to face whatever challenges come our way when we choose to proclaim that God is the best.

How does recognizing that God is the best help us deal with feelings of uncertainty or loneliness?

GOD IS
THE BEST

What is one thing you can do in your daily life to live like God is the best?

PSALM 95

What specific verses in Psalm 95 emphasize the greatness and power of God?

Exasperated, I exploded,
   'They'll never get where they're headed,
   never be able to sit down and rest.'"

1-2 **96** Sing GOD a brand-new song!
           Earth and everyone in it, sing!
Sing to GOD—*worship* GOD!

2-3 Shout the news of his victory from sea to sea,
   Take the news of his glory to the lost,
   News of his wonders to one and all!

4-5 For GOD is great, and worth a thousand Hallelujahs.
   His furious beauty puts the other gods to shame;
   Pagan gods are mere tatters and rags.

5-6 GOD made the heavens—
   Royal splendor radiates from him,
   A powerful beauty sets him apart.

7 Bravo, GOD, Bravo!
   Everyone join in the great shout: Encore!
   In awe before the beauty, in awe before
       the might.

8-9 Bring gifts and celebrate,
   Bow before the beauty of GOD,
   Then to your knees—everyone worship!

10 Get out the message—GOD Rules!
   He put the world on a firm foundation;
   He treats everyone fair and square.

11 Let's hear it from Sky,
   With Earth joining in,
   And a huge round of applause from Sea.

12 Let Wilderness turn cartwheels,
   Animals, come dance,
   Put every tree of the forest in the choir—

13 An extravaganza before GOD as he comes,
   As he comes to set everything right on earth,
   Set everything right, treat everyone fair.

1 **97** GOD rules: *there's* something to shout over!
           On the double, mainlands and islands—celebrate!

2 Bright clouds and storm clouds circle 'round him;
   Right and justice anchor his rule.

Fire blazes out before him,   3
Flaming high up the craggy mountains.

His lightnings light up the world;   4
Earth, wide-eyed, trembles in fear.

The mountains take one look at GOD   5
And melt, melt like wax before earth's Lord.

The heavens announce that he'll set everything right,   6
And everyone will see it happen—glorious!

All who serve handcrafted gods will be sorry—   •   7-8
And they were so proud of their ragamuffin gods!

On your knees, all you gods—worship him!
And Zion, you listen and take heart!

Daughters of Zion, sing your hearts out:
GOD has done it all, has set everything right.

You, GOD, are High God of the cosmos,   9
Far, far higher than any of the gods.

GOD loves all who hate evil,   10
And those who love him he keeps safe,
Snatches them from the grip of the wicked.

Light-seeds are planted in the souls of God's people,   11
Joy-seeds are planted in good heart-soil.

So, God's people, shout praise to GOD,   12
Give thanks to our Holy God!

98 Sing to GOD a brand-new song.   1
He's made a world of wonders!

He rolled up his sleeves,
He set things right.

GOD made history with salvation,   2
He showed the world what he could do.

He remembered to love us, a bonus   3
To his dear family, Israel—indefatigable love.

The whole earth comes to attention.
Look—God's work of salvation!

Shout your praises to GOD, everybody!   4
Let loose and sing! Strike up the band!

5 Round up an orchestra to play for GOD,
    Add on a hundred-voice choir.

6 Feature trumpets and big trombones,
    Fill the air with praises to King GOD.

7 Let the sea and its fish give a round of applause,
    With everything living on earth joining in.

8 Let ocean breakers call out, "Encore!"
    And mountains harmonize the finale—

9 A tribute to GOD when he comes,
    When he comes to set the earth right.

    He'll straighten out the whole world,
    He'll put the world right, and everyone in it.

1-3 **99** GOD rules. On your toes, everybody!
        He rules from his angel throne—take notice!
    GOD looms majestic in Zion,
    He towers in splendor over all the big names.
    Great and terrible your beauty: let everyone praise you!
        Holy. Yes, holy.

4-5 Strong King, lover of justice,
    You laid things out fair and square;
    You set down the foundations in Jacob,
    Foundation stones of just and right ways.
    Honor GOD, our God; worship his rule!
        Holy. Yes, holy.

6-9 Moses and Aaron were his priests,
    Samuel among those who prayed to him.
    They prayed to GOD and he answered them;
    He spoke from the pillar of cloud.
    And they did what he said; they kept the law he
            gave them.
    And then GOD, our God, answered them
    (But you were never soft on their sins).
    Lift high GOD, our God; worship at his holy mountain.
        Holy. Yes, holy is GOD our God.

A THANKSGIVING PSALM

1-2 **100** On your feet now—applaud GOD!
        Bring a gift of laughter,
    sing yourselves into his presence.

3 Know this: GOD is God, and God, GOD.
    He made us; we didn't make him.
    We're his people, his well-tended sheep.

LOVE THROUGH CONSEQUENCES

If we aren't careful, we can think that love and consequences never go together. But consequences are one of the ways we experience God's love. God has set up the world in such a way that many of our wrong decisions cause negative consequences. Experiencing a consequence for doing something wrong helps us learn to do what is right. This form of God's love is written into the very nature of existence. While it may be hard to take, seeing God's heart for us through consequences can be one of the most helpful and formative ways we experience God's love.

1 What do you notice about God as a ruler in this psalm?

PSALM 99

2 Where do you see God's love most in this chapter?

3 When have you experienced God's love through consequences?

4 Enter with the password: "Thank you!"
  Make yourselves at home, talking praise.
  Thank him. Worship him.

5 For GOD is sheer beauty,
  all-generous in love,
  loyal always and ever.

A DAVID PSALM

1-8 **101** My theme song is God's love and justice,
         and I'm singing it right to you, GOD.
I'm finding my way down the road of right living,
  but how long before you show up?
I'm doing the very best I can,
  and I'm doing it at home, where it counts.
I refuse to take a second look
  at corrupting people and degrading things.
I reject made-in-Canaan gods,
  stay clear of contamination.
The crooked in heart keep their distance;
  I refuse to shake hands with those who plan evil.
I put a gag on the gossip
  who bad-mouths his neighbor;
I can't stand
  arrogance.
But I have my eye on salt-of-the-earth people—
  they're the ones I want working with me;
Men and women on the straight and narrow—
  these are the ones I want at my side.
But no one who traffics in lies
  gets a job with me; I have no patience with liars.
I've rounded up all the wicked like cattle
  and herded them right out of the country.
I purged GOD's city
  of all who make a business of evil.

A PRAYER OF ONE WHOSE LIFE IS FALLING TO PIECES, AND WHO LETS GOD KNOW JUST HOW BAD IT IS

1-2 **102** GOD, listen! Listen to my prayer,
         listen to the pain in my cries.
Don't turn your back on me
  just when I need you so desperately.
Pay attention! This is a cry for *help*!
  And hurry—this can't wait!

3-11 I'm wasting away to nothing,
  I'm burning up with fever.
I'm a ghost of my former self,
  half-consumed already by terminal illness.
My jaws ache from gritting my teeth;
  I'm nothing but skin and bones.

LOVE AND JUSTICE

2 How do the concepts of love and justice connect to each other in the context of growing up?

As you grow up, you're constantly bombarded with messages that tell you what you should believe and how you should live. It's easy to get caught up in the latest trends and forget about the things that really matter. However, if you make God's love and justice your theme song, then you'll have a solid foundation upon which you can build your life. Let God's love guide you in your relationships and God's justice move you to stand up for the oppressed and fight for what is right. As you go through your daily life, let the theme song of the love and justice of God be your guide.

PSALM 101

How does making God's love and justice your theme song help you navigate through life?

1

3 What's one way you can make God's love and justice your theme song today?

I'm like a buzzard in the desert,
    a crow perched on the rubble.
Insomniac, I twitter away,
    mournful as a sparrow in the gutter.
All day long my enemies taunt me,
    while others just curse.
They bring in meals—casseroles of ashes!
    I draw drink from a barrel of my tears.
And all because of your furious anger;
    you swept me up and threw me out.
There's nothing left of me—
    a withered weed, swept clean from the path.

12-17 Yet you, GOD, are sovereign still,
    always and ever sovereign.
You'll get up from your throne and help Zion—
    it's time for compassionate help.
Oh, how your servants love this city's rubble
    and weep with compassion over its dust!
The godless nations will sit up and take notice
    —see your glory, worship your name—
When GOD rebuilds Zion,
    when he shows up in all his glory,
When he attends to the prayer of the wretched.
    He won't dismiss their prayer.

18-22 Write this down for the next generation
    so people not yet born will praise GOD:
"GOD looked out from his high holy place;
    from heaven he surveyed the earth.
He listened to the groans of the doomed,
    he opened the doors of their death cells."
Write it so the story can be told in Zion,
    so GOD's praise will be sung in Jerusalem's
        streets
And wherever people gather together
    along with their rulers to worship him.

23-28 GOD sovereignly brought me to my knees,
    he cut me down in my prime.
"Oh, don't," I prayed, "please don't let me die.
    You have more years than you know what to
        do with!
You laid earth's foundations a long time ago,
    and handcrafted the very heavens;
You'll still be around when they're long gone,
    threadbare and discarded like an old suit of clothes.
You'll throw them away like a worn-out coat,
    but year after year you're as good as new.
Your servants' children will have a good place to live
    and their children will be at home with you."

A DAVID PSALM

103

O my soul, bless GOD.   1-2
From head to toe, I'll bless his holy name!
O my soul, bless GOD,
    don't forget a single blessing!

He forgives your sins—every one.   3-5
He heals your diseases—every one.
He redeems you from hell—saves your life!
He crowns you with love and mercy—a paradise
        crown.
He wraps you in goodness—beauty eternal.
He renews your youth—you're always young in
        his presence.

GOD makes everything come out right;   6-18
    he puts victims back on their feet.
He showed Moses how he went about his work,
    opened up his plans to all Israel.
GOD is sheer mercy and grace;
    not easily angered, he's rich in love.
He doesn't endlessly nag and scold,
    nor hold grudges forever.
He doesn't treat us as our sins deserve,
    nor pay us back in full for our wrongs.
As high as heaven is over the earth,
    so strong is his love to those who fear him.
And as far as sunrise is from sunset,
    he has separated us from our sins.
As parents feel for their children,
    GOD feels for those who fear him.
He knows us inside and out,
    keeps in mind that we're made of mud.
Men and women don't live very long;
    like wildflowers they spring up and blossom,
But a storm snuffs them out just as quickly,
    leaving nothing to show they were here.
GOD's love, though, is ever and always,
    eternally present to all who fear him,
Making everything right for them and their children
    as they follow his Covenant ways
    and remember to do whatever he said.

GOD has set his throne in heaven;   19-22
    he rules over us all. He's the King!
So bless GOD, you angels,
    ready and able to fly at his bidding,
    quick to hear and do what he says.
Bless GOD, all you armies of angels,
    alert to respond to whatever he wills.

Bless God, all creatures, wherever you are—
   everything and everyone made by God.

And you, O my soul, bless God!

1-14   **104**   O my soul, bless God!

God, my God, how great you are!
   beautifully, gloriously robed,
Dressed up in sunshine,
   and all heaven stretched out for your tent.
You built your palace on the ocean deeps,
   made a chariot out of clouds and took off on wind-wings.
You commandeered winds as messengers,
   appointed fire and flame as ambassadors.
You set earth on a firm foundation
   so that nothing can shake it, ever.
You blanketed earth with ocean,
   covered the mountains with deep waters;
Then you roared and the water ran away—
   your thunder crash put it to flight.
Mountains pushed up, valleys spread out
   in the places you assigned them.
You set boundaries between earth and sea;
   never again will earth be flooded.
You started the springs and rivers,
   sent them flowing among the hills.
All the wild animals now drink their fill,
   wild donkeys quench their thirst.
Along the riverbanks the birds build nests,
   ravens make their voices heard.
You water the mountains from your heavenly reservoirs;
   earth is supplied with plenty of water.
You make grass grow for the livestock,
   hay for the animals that plow the ground.

14-23   Oh yes, God brings grain from the land,
   wine to make people happy,
Their faces glowing with health,
   a people well-fed and hearty.
God's trees are well-watered—
   the Lebanon cedars he planted.
Birds build their nests in those trees;
   look—the stork at home in the treetop.
Mountain goats climb about the cliffs;
   badgers burrow among the rocks.
The moon keeps track of the seasons,
   the sun is in charge of each day.
When it's dark and night takes over,
   all the forest creatures come out.

The young lions roar for their prey,
    clamoring to God for their supper.
When the sun comes up, they vanish,
    lazily stretched out in their dens.
Meanwhile, men and women go out to work,
    busy at their jobs until evening.

What a wildly wonderful world, GOD!   24-30
    You made it all, with Wisdom at your side,
    made earth overflow with your wonderful creations.
Oh, look—the deep, wide sea,
    brimming with fish past counting,
    sardines and sharks and salmon.
Ships plow those waters,
    and Leviathan, your pet dragon, romps in them.
All the creatures look expectantly to you
    to give them their meals on time.
You come, and they gather around;
    you open your hand and they eat from it.
If you turned your back,
    they'd die in a minute—
Take back your Spirit and they die,
    revert to original mud;
Send out your Spirit and they spring to life—
    the whole countryside in bloom and blossom.

The glory of GOD—let it last forever!   31-32
    Let GOD enjoy his creation!
He takes one look at earth and triggers an earthquake,
    points a finger at the mountains, and volcanoes erupt.

Oh, let me sing to GOD all my life long,   33-35
    sing hymns to my God as long as I live!
Oh, let my song please him;
    I'm so pleased to be singing to GOD.
But clear the ground of sinners—
    no more godless men and women!

O my soul, bless GOD!

105 Hallelujah!   1-6

Thank GOD! Pray to him by name!
    Tell everyone you meet what he has done!
Sing him songs, belt out hymns,
    translate his wonders into music!
Honor his holy name with Hallelujahs,
    you who seek GOD. Live a happy life!
Keep your eyes open for GOD, watch for his works;
    be alert for signs of his presence.

Remember the world of wonders he has made,
    his miracles, and the verdicts he's rendered—
      O seed of Abraham, his servant,
      O child of Jacob, his chosen.

7-15 He's GOD, our God,
    in charge of the whole earth.
And he remembers, remembers his Covenant—
    for a thousand generations he's been as good as
      his word.
It's the Covenant he made with Abraham,
    the same oath he swore to Isaac,
The very statute he established with Jacob,
    the eternal Covenant with Israel,
Namely, "I give you the land.
    Canaan is your hill-country inheritance."
When they didn't count for much,
    a mere handful, and strangers at that,
Wandering from country to country,
    drifting from pillar to post,
He permitted no one to abuse them.
    He told kings to keep their hands off:
"Don't you dare lay a hand on my anointed,
    don't hurt a hair on the heads of my prophets."

16-22 Then he called down a famine on the country,
    he broke every last blade of wheat.
But he sent a man on ahead:
    Joseph, sold as a slave.
They put cruel chains on his ankles,
    an iron collar around his neck,
Until God's word came to the Pharaoh,
    and GOD confirmed his promise.
God sent the king to release him.
    The Pharaoh set Joseph free;
He appointed him master of his palace,
    put him in charge of all his business
To personally instruct his princes
    and train his advisors in wisdom.

23-42 Then Israel entered Egypt,
    Jacob immigrated to the Land of Ham.
God gave his people lots of babies;
    soon their numbers alarmed their foes.
He turned the Egyptians against his people;
    they abused and cheated God's servants.
Then he sent his servant Moses,
    and Aaron, whom he also chose.
They worked marvels in that spiritual wasteland,
    miracles in the Land of Ham.

He spoke, "Darkness!" and it turned dark—
   they couldn't see what they were doing.
He turned all their water to blood
   so that all their fish died;
He made frogs swarm through the land,
   even into the king's bedroom;
He gave the word and flies swarmed,
   gnats filled the air.
He substituted hail for rain,
   he stabbed their land with lightning;
He wasted their vines and fig trees,
   smashed their groves of trees to splinters;
With a word he brought in locusts,
   millions of locusts, armies of locusts;
They consumed every blade of grass in the country
   and picked the ground clean of produce;
He struck down every firstborn in the land,
   the first fruits of their virile powers.
He led Israel out, their arms filled with loot,
   and not one among his tribes even stumbled.
Egypt was glad to have them go—
   they were scared to death of them.
God spread a cloud to keep them cool through
     the day
   and a fire to light their way through the night;
They prayed and he brought quail,
   filled them with the bread of heaven;
He opened the rock and water poured out;
   it flowed like a river through that desert—
All because he remembered his Covenant,
   his promise to Abraham, his servant.

Remember this! He led his people out singing for joy;   43-45
   his chosen people marched, singing their hearts out!
He made them a gift of the country they entered,
   helped them seize the wealth of the nations
So they could do everything he told them—
   could follow his instructions to the letter.

Hallelujah!

106
Hallelujah!   1-3
Thank GOD! And why?
  Because he's good, because his love lasts.
But who on earth can do it—
   declaim GOD's mighty acts, broadcast all his praises?
You're one happy man when you do what's right,
   one happy woman when you form the habit of justice.

Remember me, GOD, when you enjoy your people;   4-5
   include me when you save them;

I want to see your chosen succeed,
　　celebrate with your celebrating nation,
　　join the Hallelujahs of your pride and joy!

6-12　We've sinned a lot, both we and our parents;
　　We've fallen short, hurt a lot of people.
After our parents left Egypt,
　　they took your wonders for granted,
　　forgot your great and wonderful love.
They were barely beyond the Red Sea
　　when they defied the High God
　　—the very place he saved them!
　　—the place he revealed his amazing power!
He rebuked the Red Sea so that it dried up on the spot
　　—he paraded them right through!
　　—no one so much as got wet feet!
He saved them from a life of oppression,
　　pried them loose from the grip of the enemy.
Then the waters flowed back on their oppressors;
　　there wasn't a single survivor.
Then they believed his words were true
　　and broke out in songs of praise.

13-18　But it wasn't long before they forgot the whole thing,
　　wouldn't wait to be told what to do.
They only cared about pleasing themselves in that desert,
　　provoked God with their insistent demands.
He gave them exactly what they asked for—
　　but along with it they got an empty heart.
One day in camp some grew jealous of Moses,
　　also of Aaron, holy priest of GOD.
The ground opened and swallowed Dathan,
　　then buried Abiram's gang.
Fire flared against that rebel crew
　　and torched them to a cinder.

19-22　They cast in metal a bull calf at Horeb
　　and worshiped the statue they'd made.
They traded the Glory
　　for a cheap piece of sculpture—a grass-chewing bull!
They forgot God, their very own Savior,
　　who turned things around in Egypt,
Who created a world of wonders in the Land of Ham,
　　who gave that stunning performance at the Red Sea.

23-27　Fed up, God decided to get rid of them—
　　and except for Moses, his chosen, he would have.
But Moses stood in the gap and deflected God's anger,
　　prevented it from destroying them utterly.
They went on to reject the Blessed Land,
　　didn't believe a word of what God promised.

They found fault with the life they had
    and turned a deaf ear to GOD's voice.
Exasperated, God swore
    that he'd lay them low in the desert,
Scattering their children here and there,
    strewing them all over the earth.

Then they linked up with Baal Peor,   28-31
    attending funeral banquets and eating idol food.
That made God so angry
    that a plague spread through their ranks;
Phinehas stood up and pled their case
    and the plague was stopped.
This was counted to his credit;
    his descendants will never forget it.

They angered God again at Meribah Springs;   32-33
    this time Moses got mixed up in their evil;
Because they defied GOD yet again,
    Moses exploded and lost his temper.

They didn't wipe out those godless cultures   34-39
    as ordered by GOD;
Instead they intermarried with the heathen,
    and in time became just like them.
They worshiped their idols,
    were caught in the trap of idols.
They sacrificed their sons and daughters
    at the altars of demon gods.
They slit the throats of their babies,
    murdered their infant girls and boys.
They offered their babies to Canaan's gods;
    the blood of their babies stained the land.
Their way of life reeked;
    they lived like prostitutes.

And GOD was furious—a wildfire anger;   40-43
    he couldn't stand even to look at his people.
He turned them over to the heathen
    so that the people who hated them ruled them.
Their enemies made life hard for them;
    they were tyrannized under that rule.
Over and over God rescued them, but they never learned—
    until finally their sins destroyed them.

Still, when God saw the trouble they were in   44-46
    and heard their cries for help,
He remembered his Covenant with them,
    and, immense with love, took them by the hand.
He poured out his mercy on them
    while their captors looked on, amazed.

47-48 Save us, GOD, our God!
    Gather us back out of exile
So we can give thanks to your holy name
    and join in the glory when you are praised!

    Blessed be GOD, Israel's God!
    Bless now, bless always!
    Oh! Let everyone say Amen!
    Hallelujah!

1-3 **107** Oh, thank GOD—he's so good!
    His love never runs out.
All of you set free by GOD, tell the world!
    Tell how he freed you from oppression,
Then rounded you up from all over the place,
    from the four winds, from the seven seas.

4-9 Some of you wandered for years in the desert,
    looking but not finding a good place to live,
Half-starved and parched with thirst,
    staggering and stumbling, on the brink of exhaustion.
Then, in your desperate condition, you called out to GOD.
    He got you out in the nick of time;
He put your feet on a wonderful road
    that took you straight to a good place to live.
So thank GOD for his marvelous love,
    for his miracle mercy to the children he loves.
He poured great drafts of water down parched throats;
    the starved and hungry got plenty to eat.

10-16 Some of you were locked in a dark cell,
    cruelly confined behind bars,
Punished for defying God's Word,
    for turning your back on the High God's counsel—
A hard sentence, and your hearts so heavy,
    and not a soul in sight to help.
Then you called out to GOD in your desperate condition;
    he got you out in the nick of time.
He led you out of your dark, dark cell,
    broke open the jail and led you out.
So thank GOD for his marvelous love,
    for his miracle mercy to the children he loves;
He shattered the heavy jailhouse doors,
    he snapped the prison bars like matchsticks!

17-22 Some of you were sick because you'd lived a bad life,
    your bodies feeling the effects of your sin;
You couldn't stand the sight of food,
    so miserable you thought you'd be better off dead.
Then you called out to GOD in your desperate condition;
    he got you out in the nick of time.

He spoke the word that healed you,
    that pulled you back from the brink of death.
So thank GOD for his marvelous love,
    for his miracle mercy to the children he loves;
Offer thanksgiving sacrifices,
    tell the world what he's done—sing it out!

Some of you set sail in big ships;
    you put to sea to do business in faraway ports.
Out at sea you saw GOD in action,
    saw his breathtaking ways with the ocean:
With a word he called up the wind—
    an ocean storm, towering waves!
You shot high in the sky, then the bottom dropped out;
    your hearts were stuck in your throats.
You were spun like a top, you reeled like a drunk,
    you didn't know which end was up.
Then you called out to GOD in your desperate condition;
    he got you out in the nick of time.
He quieted the wind down to a whisper,
    put a muzzle on all the big waves.
And you were so glad when the storm died down,
    and he led you safely back to harbor.
So thank GOD for his marvelous love,
    for his miracle mercy to the children he loves.
Lift high your praises when the people assemble,
    shout Hallelujah when the elders meet!

23-32

GOD turned rivers into wasteland,
    springs of water into sunbaked mud;
Luscious orchards became alkali flats
    because of the evil of the people who lived there.
Then he changed wasteland into fresh pools
      of water,
    arid earth into springs of water,
Brought in the hungry and settled them there;
    they moved in—what a great place to live!
They sowed the fields, they planted vineyards,
    they reaped a bountiful harvest.
He blessed them and they prospered greatly;
    their herds of cattle never decreased.
But abuse and evil and trouble declined
    as he heaped scorn on princes and sent them away.
He gave the poor a safe place to live,
    treated their clans like well-cared-for sheep.

33-41

Good people see this and are glad;
    bad people are speechless, stopped in their tracks.
If you are really wise, you'll think this over—
    it's time you appreciated GOD's deep love.

42-43

Whether you find yourself lost in the wilderness, in need of healing, or caught in the storms of life, God is always ready to save you "in the nick of time" (Psalm 107:6). As you go through life, you may face challenges that seem unbeatable. You may feel alone, afraid, or uncertain of your future. But the good news is that God is with you every step of the way. In every situation, remember that God is your ever-present help, ready to come to your aid in the nick of time. May this truth bring peace to your heart and comfort to your soul.

3 What is one way you can actively trust God during challenging situations?

IN THE NICK OF TIME

2 In your own words, describe what "in the nick of time" means.

PSALM 107

How does Psalm 107 describe God's love and faithfulness toward us? **1**

A DAVID PRAYER

108 I'm ready, God, so ready,
    ready from head to toe.
Ready to sing,
    ready to raise a God-song:
"Wake, soul! Wake, lute!
    Wake up, you sleepyhead sun!"

1-2

I'm thanking you, GOD, out in the streets,
    singing your praises in town and country.
The deeper your love, the higher it goes;
    every cloud's a flag to your faithfulness.
Soar high in the skies, O God!
    Cover the whole earth with your glory!
And for the sake of the one you love so much,
    reach down and help me—answer me!

3-6

That's when God spoke in holy splendor:
    "Brimming over with joy,
I make a present of Shechem,
    I hand out Succoth Valley as a gift.
Gilead's in my pocket,
    to say nothing of Manasseh.
Ephraim's my hard hat,
    Judah my hammer.
Moab's a scrub bucket—
    I mop the floor with Moab,
Spit on Edom,
    rain fireworks all over Philistia."

7-9

Who will take me to the thick of the fight?
    Who'll show me the road to Edom?
You aren't giving up on us, are you, God?
    refusing to go out with our troops?

10-11

Give us help for the hard task;
    human help is worthless.
In God we'll do our very best;
    he'll flatten the opposition for good.

12-13

A DAVID PRAYER

109 My God, don't turn a deaf ear to my hallelujah prayer.
    Liars are pouring out invective on me;
Their lying tongues are like a pack of dogs out to get me,
    barking their hate, nipping my heels—
        and for no reason!
I loved them and now they slander me—yes, me!—
    and treat my prayer like a crime;
They return my good with evil,
    they return my love with hate.

1-5

6-20 Send the Evil One to accuse my accusing judge;
          dispatch Satan to prosecute him.
       When he's judged, let the verdict be "Guilty,"
          and when he prays, let his prayer turn to sin.
       Give him a short life,
          and give his job to somebody else.
       Make orphans of his children,
          dress his wife in widow's black;
       Turn his children into begging street urchins,
          evicted from their homes—homeless.
       May the bank foreclose and wipe him out,
          and strangers, like vultures, pick him clean.
       May there be no one around to help him out,
          no one willing to give his orphans a break.
       Chop down his family tree
          so that nobody even remembers his name.
       But erect a memorial to the sin of his father,
          and make sure his mother's name is there, too—
       Their sins recorded forever before GOD,
          but they themselves sunk in oblivion.
       That's all he deserves since he was never once kind,
          hounded the afflicted and heartbroken to their graves.
       Since he loved cursing so much,
          let curses rain down;
       Since he had no taste for blessing,
          let blessings flee far from him.
       He dressed up in curses like a fine suit of clothes;
          he drank curses, took his baths in curses.
       So give him a gift—a costume of curses;
          he can wear curses every day of the week!
       That's what they'll get, those out to get me—
          an avalanche of just deserts from GOD.

21-25 Oh, GOD, my Lord, step in;
          work a miracle for me—you can do it!
       Get me out of here—your love is so great!—
          I'm at the end of my rope, my life in ruins.
       I'm fading away to nothing, passing away,
          my youth gone, old before my time.
       I'm weak from hunger and can hardly stand up,
          my body a rack of skin and bones.
       I'm a joke in poor taste to those who see me;
          they take one look and shake their heads.

26-29 Help me, oh help me, GOD, my God,
          save me through your wonderful love;
       Then they'll know that your hand is in this,
          that you, GOD, have been at work.
       Let them curse all they want;
          you do the blessing.

Let them be jeered by the crowd when they stand up,
    followed by cheers for me, your servant.
Dress my accusers in clothes dirty with shame,
    discarded and humiliating old ragbag clothes.

My mouth's full of great praise for GOD,   30-31
    I'm singing his hallelujahs surrounded by crowds,
For he's always at hand to take the side of the needy,
    to rescue a life from the unjust judge.

A DAVID PRAYER

110 The word of GOD to my Lord: 1-3
    "Sit alongside me here on my throne
until I make your enemies a stool for your feet."
You were forged a strong scepter by GOD of Zion;
    now rule, though surrounded by enemies!
Your people will freely join you, resplendent in holy armor
    on the great day of your conquest,
Join you at the fresh break of day,
    join you with all the vigor of youth.

GOD gave his word and he won't take it back: 4-7
    you're the permanent priest, the Melchizedek priest.
The Lord stands true at your side,
    crushing kings in his terrible wrath,
Bringing judgment on the nations,
    handing out convictions wholesale,
    crushing opposition across the wide earth.
The King-Maker put his King on the throne;
    the True King rules with head held high!

111 Hallelujah!   1-10
    I give thanks to GOD with everything I've got—
Wherever good people gather, and in the congregation.
GOD's works are so great, worth
A lifetime of study—endless enjoyment!
Splendor and beauty mark his craft;
His generosity never gives out.
His miracles are his memorial—
This GOD of Grace, this GOD of Love.
He gave food to those who fear him,
He remembered to keep his ancient promise.
He proved to his people that he could do what he said:
Hand them the nations on a platter—a gift!
He manufactures truth and justice;
All his products are guaranteed to last—
Never out-of-date, never obsolete, rust-proof.
All that he makes and does is honest and true:
He paid the ransom for his people,
He ordered his Covenant kept forever.

He's so personal and holy, worthy of our respect.
The good life begins in the fear of GOD—
Do that and you'll know the blessing of GOD.
His Hallelujah lasts forever!

1-10 **112** Hallelujah!
Blessed man, blessed woman, who fear GOD,
Who cherish and relish his commandments,
Their children robust on the earth,
And the homes of the upright—how blessed!
Their houses brim with wealth
And a generosity that never runs dry.
Sunrise breaks through the darkness for good people—
God's grace and mercy and justice!
The good person is generous and lends lavishly;
No shuffling or stumbling around for this one,
But a sterling and solid and lasting reputation.
Unfazed by rumor and gossip,
Heart ready, trusting in GOD,
Spirit firm, unperturbed,
Ever blessed, relaxed among enemies,
They lavish gifts on the poor—
A generosity that goes on, and on, and on.
An honored life! A beautiful life!
Someone wicked takes one look and rages,
Blusters away but ends up speechless.
There's nothing to the dreams of the wicked. Nothing.

1-3 **113** Hallelujah!
You who serve GOD, praise GOD!
Just to speak his name is praise!
Just to remember GOD is a blessing—
now and tomorrow and always.
From east to west, from dawn to dusk,
keep lifting all your praises to GOD!

4-9 GOD is higher than anything and anyone,
outshining everything you can see in the skies.
Who can compare with GOD, our God,
so majestically enthroned,
Surveying his magnificent
heavens and earth?
He picks up the poor from out of the dirt,
rescues the forgotten who've been thrown out with
the trash,
Seats them among the honored guests,
a place of honor among the brightest and best.
He gives childless couples a family,
gives them joy as the parents of children.
Hallelujah!

GOD RESCUES THE FORGOTTEN

Have you ever wondered whether God cares about people the world seems to have forgotten—the unhoused, the immigrant or refugee, the person without any family? You may even feel forgotten sometimes; feeling insignificant or unnoticed is an experience all humans share. If you're worried that God only cares for the wealthy, powerful, or famous, let this psalm remind you that God is the God of the poor, the forgotten, and the oppressed. This psalmist affirms that God rescues the forgotten and raises the poor from the pile of dust. We can take heart that God sees us, cares for us, and will rescue us from any situation we may find ourselves in.

PSALM 113

How do the qualities of God mentioned in Psalm 113 make you feel about your own worth and significance?

How does God's care for the marginalized change your own attitude and action toward those who may be overlooked or forgotten in our world?

What's one way you can demonstrate God's love for the less fortunate in your day-to-day life?

1-8 **114** After Israel left Egypt,
  the clan of Jacob left those barbarians behind;
Judah became holy land for him,
  Israel the place of holy rule.
Sea took one look and ran the other way;
  River Jordan turned around and ran off.
The mountains turned playful and skipped like rams,
  the hills frolicked like spring lambs.
What's wrong with you, Sea, that you ran away?
  and you, River Jordan, that you turned and ran off?
And mountains, why did you skip like rams?
  and you, hills, frolic like spring lambs?
Tremble, Earth! You're in the Lord's presence!
  in the presence of Jacob's God.
He turned the rock into a pool of cool water,
  turned flint into fresh spring water.

1-2 **115** Not for our sake, GOD, no, not for our sake,
  but for your name's sake, show your glory.
Do it on account of your merciful love,
  do it on account of your faithful ways.
Do it so none of the nations can say,
  "Where now, oh where is their God?"

3-8 Our God is in heaven
  doing whatever he wants to do.
Their gods are metal and wood,
  handmade in a basement shop:
Carved mouths that can't talk,
  painted eyes that can't see,
Tin ears that can't hear,
  molded noses that can't smell,
Hands that can't grasp, feet that can't walk or run,
  throats that never utter a sound.
Those who make them have become just like them,
  have become just like the gods they trust.

9-11 But you, Israel: put your trust in GOD!
  —trust your Helper! trust your Ruler!
Clan of Aaron, trust in GOD!
  —trust your Helper! trust your Ruler!
You who fear GOD, trust in GOD!
  —trust your Helper! trust your Ruler!

12-16 O GOD, remember us and bless us,
  bless the families of Israel and Aaron.
And let GOD bless all who fear GOD—
  bless the small, bless the great.
Oh, let GOD enlarge your families—
  giving growth to you, growth to your children.

May you be blessed by GOD,
   by GOD, who made heaven and earth.
The heaven of heavens is for GOD,
   but he put us in charge of the earth.

Dead people can't praise GOD—   17-18
   not a word to be heard from those buried in the ground.
But we bless GOD, oh yes—
   we bless him now, we bless him always!
Hallelujah!

116   I love GOD because he listened to me,   1-6
      listened as I begged for mercy.
He listened so intently
   as I laid out my case before him.
Death stared me in the face,
   hell was hard on my heels.
Up against it, I didn't know which way to turn;
   then I called out to GOD for help:
"Please, GOD!" I cried out.
   "Save my life!"
GOD is gracious—it is he who makes things right,
   our most compassionate God.
GOD takes the side of the helpless;
   when I was at the end of my rope, he saved me.

I said to myself, "Relax and rest.   7-8
   GOD has showered you with blessings.
Soul, you've been rescued from death;
Eye, you've been rescued from tears;
And you, Foot, were kept from stumbling."

I'm striding in the presence of GOD,   9-11
   alive in the land of the living!
I stayed faithful, though overwhelmed,
   and despite a ton of bad luck,
Despite giving up on the human race,
   saying, "They're all liars and cheats."

What can I give back to GOD   12-19
   for the blessings he's poured out on me?
I'll lift high the cup of salvation—a toast to GOD!
   I'll pray in the name of GOD;
I'll complete what I promised GOD I'd do,
   and I'll do it together with his people.
When they arrive at the gates of death,
   GOD welcomes those who love him.
Oh, GOD, here I am, your servant,
   your faithful servant: set me free for your service!
I'm ready to offer the thanksgiving sacrifice
   and pray in the name of GOD.

I'll complete what I promised GOD I'd do,
    and I'll do it in company with his people,
In the place of worship, in GOD's house,
    in Jerusalem, GOD's city.
Hallelujah!

1-2 **117** Praise GOD, everybody!
    Applaud GOD, all people!
His love has taken over our lives;
GOD's faithful ways are eternal.
    Hallelujah!

1-4 **118** Thank GOD because he's good,
    because his love never quits.
Tell the world, Israel,
    "His love never quits."
And you, clan of Aaron, tell the world,
    "His love never quits."
And you who fear GOD, join in,
    "His love never quits."

5-16 Pushed to the wall, I called to GOD;
    from the wide open spaces, he answered.
GOD's now at my side and I'm not afraid;
    who would dare lay a hand on me?
GOD's my strong champion;
    I flick off my enemies like flies.
Far better to take refuge in GOD
    than trust in people;
Far better to take refuge in GOD
    than trust in celebrities.
Hemmed in by barbarians,
    in GOD's name I rubbed their faces in the dirt;
Hemmed in and with no way out,
    in GOD's name I rubbed their faces in the dirt;
Like swarming bees, like wild prairie fire, they hemmed
    me in;
    in GOD's name I rubbed their faces in the dirt.
I was right on the cliff-edge, ready to fall,
    when GOD grabbed and held me.
GOD's my strength, he's also my song,
    and now he's my salvation.
Hear the shouts, hear the triumph songs
    in the camp of the saved?
      "The hand of GOD has turned the tide!
      The hand of GOD is raised in victory!
      The hand of GOD has turned the tide!"

17-20 I didn't die. I *lived*!
    And now I'm telling the world what
      GOD did.

GOD tested me, he pushed me hard,
  but he didn't hand me over to Death.
Swing wide the city gates—the *righteous* gates!
  I'll walk right through and thank GOD!
This Temple Gate belongs to GOD,
  so the victors can enter and praise.

Thank you for responding to me;   21-25
  you've truly become my salvation!
The stone the masons discarded as flawed
  is now the capstone!
This is GOD's work.
  We rub our eyes—we can hardly believe it!
This is the very day GOD acted—
  let's celebrate and be festive!
Salvation now, GOD. Salvation now!
  Oh yes, GOD—a free and full life!

Blessed are you who enter in GOD's name—   26-29
  from GOD's house we bless you!
GOD is God,
  he has bathed us in light.
Adorn the shrine with garlands,
  hang colored banners above the altar!
You're my God, and I thank you.
  O my God, I lift high your praise.
Thank GOD—he's so good.
  His love never quits!

119 You're blessed when you stay on course,   1-8
    walking steadily on the road revealed by GOD.
You're blessed when you follow his directions,
  doing your best to find him.
That's right—you don't go off on your own;
  you walk straight along the road he set.
You, GOD, prescribed the right way to live;
  now you expect us to live it.
Oh, that my steps might be steady,
  keeping to the course you set;
Then I'd never have any regrets
  in comparing my life with your counsel.
I thank you for speaking straight from your heart;
  I learn the pattern of your righteous ways.
I'm going to do what you tell me to do;
  don't ever walk off and leave me.

+ + +

How can a young person live a clean life?   9-16
  By carefully reading the map of
    your Word.

I'm single-minded in pursuit of you;
   don't let me miss the road signs you've posted.
I've banked your promises in the vault of my heart
   so I won't sin myself bankrupt.
Be blessed, GOD;
   train me in your ways of wise living.
I'll transfer to my lips
   all the counsel that comes from your mouth;
I delight far more in what you tell me about living
   than in gathering a pile of riches.
I ponder every morsel of wisdom from you,
   I attentively watch how you've done it.
I relish everything you've told me of life,
   I won't forget a word of it.

✦   ✦   ✦

17-24 Be generous with me and I'll live a full life;
   not for a minute will I take my eyes off your road.
Open my eyes so I can see
   what you show me of your miracle-wonders.
I'm a stranger in these parts;
   give me clear directions.
My soul is starved and hungry, ravenous!—
   insatiable for your nourishing commands.
And those who think they know so much,
   ignoring everything you tell them—let them have it!
Don't let them mock and humiliate me;
   I've been careful to do just what you said.
While bad neighbors maliciously gossip about me,
   I'm absorbed in pondering your wise counsel.
Yes, your sayings on life are what give me delight;
   I listen to them as to good neighbors!

✦   ✦   ✦

25-32 I'm feeling terrible—I couldn't feel worse!
   Get me on my feet again. You promised,
      remember?
When I told my story, you responded;
   train me well in your deep wisdom.
Help me understand these things inside and out
   so I can ponder your miracle-wonders.
My sad life's dilapidated, a falling-down barn;
   build me up again by your Word.
Barricade the road that goes Nowhere;
   grace me with your clear revelation.
I choose the true road to Somewhere,
   I post your road signs at every curve and corner.
I grasp and cling to whatever you tell me;
   GOD, don't let me down!

I'll run the course you lay out for me
   if you'll just show me how.

+   +   +

God, teach me lessons for living   33-40
   so I can stay the course.
Give me insight so I can do what you tell me—
   my whole life one long, obedient response.
Guide me down the road of your commandments;
   I love traveling this freeway!
Give me an appetite for your words of wisdom,
   and not for piling up loot.
Divert my eyes from toys and trinkets,
   invigorate me on the pilgrim way.
Affirm your promises to me—
   promises made to all who fear you.
Deflect the harsh words of my critics—
   but what you say is always so good.
See how hungry I am for your counsel;
   preserve my life through your righteous ways!

+   +   +

Let your love, God, shape my life   41-48
   with salvation, exactly as you promised;
Then I'll be able to stand up to mockery
   because I trusted your Word.
Don't ever deprive me of truth, not ever—
   your commandments are what I depend on.
Oh, I'll guard with my life what you've revealed to me,
   guard it now, guard it ever;
And I'll stride freely through wide open spaces
   as I look for your truth and your wisdom;
Then I'll tell the world what I find,
   speak out boldly in public, unembarrassed.
I cherish your commandments—oh, how I love them!—
   relishing every fragment of your counsel.

+   +   +

Remember what you said to me, your servant—   49-56
   I hang on to these words for dear life!
These words hold me up in bad times;
   yes, your promises rejuvenate me.
The haters hate me without mercy,
   but I don't budge from your revelation.
I watch for your ancient landmark words,
   and know I'm on the right track.
But when I see the wicked ignore your directions,
   I'm beside myself with anger.

I set your instructions to music
    and sing them as I walk this pilgrim way.
I meditate on your name all night, GOD,
    treasuring your revelation, O GOD.
Still, I walk through a rain of derision
    because I live by your Word and counsel.

+   +   +

57-64   Because you have satisfied me, GOD, I promise
    to do everything you say.
I beg you from the bottom of my heart: smile,
    be gracious to me just as you promised.
When I took a long, careful look at your ways,
    I got my feet back on the trail you blazed.
I was up at once, didn't drag my feet,
    was quick to follow your orders.
The wicked hemmed me in—there was no way out—
    but not for a minute did I forget your plan for me.
I get up in the middle of the night to thank you;
    your decisions are so right, so true—I can't wait till morning!
I'm a friend and companion of all who fear you,
    of those committed to living by your rules.
Your love, GOD, fills the earth!
    Train me to live by your counsel.

+   +   +

65-72   Be good to your servant, GOD;
    be as good as your Word.
Train me in good common sense;
    I'm thoroughly committed to living your way.
Before I learned to answer you, I wandered all over the place,
    but now I'm in step with your Word.
You are good, and the source of good;
    train me in your goodness.
The godless spread lies about me,
    but I focus my attention on what you are saying;
They're bland as a bucket of lard,
    while I dance to the tune of your revelation.
My troubles turned out all for the best—
    they forced me to learn from your textbook.
Truth from your mouth means more to me
    than striking it rich in a gold mine.

+   +   +

73-80   With your very own hands you formed me;
    now breathe your wisdom over me so I can understand you.
When they see me waiting, expecting your Word,
    those who fear you will take heart and be glad.

I can see now, GOD, that your decisions are right;
   your testing has taught me what's true and right.
Oh, love me—and right now!—hold me tight!
   just the way you promised.
Now comfort me so I can live, really live;
   your revelation is the tune I dance to.
Let the fast-talking tricksters be exposed as frauds;
   they tried to sell me a bill of goods,
   but I kept my mind fixed on your counsel.
Let those who fear you turn to me
   for evidence of your wise guidance.
And let me live whole and holy, soul and body,
   so I can always walk with my head held high.

+ + +

I'm homesick—longing for your salvation;   81-88
   I'm waiting for your word of hope.
My eyes grow heavy watching for some sign of
      your promise;
   how long must I wait for your comfort?
There's smoke in my eyes—they burn and water,
   but I keep a steady gaze on the instructions you post.
How long do I have to put up with all this?
   How long till you haul my tormentors into court?
The arrogant godless try to throw me off track,
   ignorant as they are of God and his ways.
Everything you command is a sure thing,
   but they harass me with lies. Help!
They've pushed and pushed—they never let up—
   but I haven't relaxed my grip on your counsel.
In your great love revive me
   so I can alertly obey your every word.

+ + +

What you say goes, GOD,   89-96
   and *stays*, as permanent as the heavens.
Your truth never goes out of fashion;
   it's as relevant as the earth when the sun comes up.
Your Word and truth are dependable as ever;
   that's what you ordered—you set the earth going.
If your revelation hadn't delighted me so,
   I would have given up when the hard times came.
But I'll never forget the advice you gave me;
   you saved my life with those wise words.
Save me! I'm all yours.
   I look high and low for your words of wisdom.
The wicked lie in ambush to destroy me,
   but I'm only concerned with your plans for me.

I see the limits to everything human,
    but the horizons can't contain your commands!

✦   ✦   ✦

97-104   Oh, how I love all you've revealed;
    I reverently ponder it all the day long.
Your commands give me an edge on my enemies;
    they never become obsolete.
I've even become smarter than my teachers
    since I've pondered and absorbed your counsel.
I've become wiser than the wise old sages
    simply by doing what you tell me.
I watch my step, avoiding the ditches and ruts
      of evil
    so I can spend all my time keeping your Word.
I never make detours from the route you laid out;
    you gave me such good directions.
Your words are so choice, so tasty;
    I prefer them to the best home cooking.
With your instruction, I understand life;
    that's why I hate false propaganda.

✦   ✦   ✦

105-112   By your words I can see where I'm going;
    they throw a beam of light on my dark path.
I've committed myself and I'll never turn back
    from living by your righteous order.
Everything's falling apart on me, GOD;
    put me together again with your Word.
Adorn me with your finest sayings, GOD;
    teach me your holy rules.
My life is as close as my own hands,
    but I don't forget what you have revealed.
The wicked do their best to throw me off track,
    but I don't swerve an inch from your course.
I inherited your book on living; it's mine forever—
    what a gift! And how happy it makes me!
I concentrate on doing exactly what you say—
    I always have and always will.

✦   ✦   ✦

113-120   I hate the two-faced,
    but I love your clear-cut revelation.
You're my place of quiet retreat;
    I wait for your Word to renew me.
Get out of my life, evildoers,
    so I can keep my God's commands.

Take my side as you promised; I'll live then for sure.
  Don't disappoint all my grand hopes.
Stick with me and I'll be all right;
  I'll give total allegiance to your definitions of life.
Expose all who drift away from your sayings;
  their casual idolatry is lethal.
You reject earth's wicked as so much rubbish;
  therefore I lovingly embrace everything you say.
I shiver in awe before you;
  your decisions leave me speechless with reverence.

+   +   +

I stood up for justice and the right;
  don't leave me to the mercy of my oppressors.
Take the side of your servant, good God;
  don't let the godless take advantage of me.
I can't keep my eyes open any longer, waiting for you
  to keep your promise to set everything right.
Let your love dictate how you deal with me;
  teach me from your textbook on life.
I'm your servant—help me understand what that means,
  the inner meaning of your instructions.
It's time to act, GOD;
  they've made a shambles of your revelation!
Yea-Saying God, I love what you command,
  I love it better than gold and gemstones;
Yea-Saying God, I honor everything you tell me,
  I despise every deceitful detour.

+   +   +

Every word you give me is a miracle word—
  how could I help but obey?
Break open your words, let the light shine out,
  let ordinary people see the meaning.
Mouth open and panting,
  I wanted your commands more than anything.
Turn my way, look kindly on me,
  as you always do to those who personally love you.
Steady my steps with your Word of promise
  so nothing malign gets the better of me.
Rescue me from the grip of bad men and women
  so I can live life your way.
Smile on me, your servant;
  teach me the right way to live.
I cry rivers of tears
  because nobody's living by your book!

+   +   +

121-128

129-136

137-144 You *are* right and you *do* right, GOD;
 your decisions are right on target.
You rightly instruct us in how to live
 ever faithful to you.
My rivals nearly did me in,
 they persistently ignored your commandments.
Your promise has been tested through and through,
 and I, your servant, love it dearly.
I'm too young to be important,
 but I don't forget what you tell me.
Your righteousness is eternally right,
 your revelation is the only truth.
Even though troubles came down on me hard,
 your commands always gave me delight.
The way you tell me to live is always right;
 help me understand it so I can live to the fullest.

+ + +

145-152 I call out at the top of my lungs,
 "GOD! Answer! I'll do whatever you say."
I called to you, "Save me
 so I can carry out all your instructions."
I was up before sunrise,
 crying for help, hoping for a word from you.
I stayed awake all night,
 prayerfully pondering your promise.
In your love, listen to me;
 in your justice, GOD, keep me alive.
As those out to get me come closer and closer,
 they go farther and farther from the truth you reveal;
But you're the closest of all to me, GOD,
 and all your judgments true.
I've known all along from the evidence of your words
 that you meant them to last forever.

+ + +

153-160 Take a good look at my trouble, and help me—
 I haven't forgotten your revelation.
Take my side and get me out of this;
 give me back my life, just as you promised.
"Salvation" is only gibberish to the wicked
 because they've never looked it up in your dictionary.
Your mercies, GOD, run into the billions;
 following your guidelines, revive me.
My antagonists are too many to count,
 but I don't swerve from the directions you gave.
I took one look at the quitters and was filled with loathing;
 they walked away from your promises so casually!

Take note of how I love what you tell me;
   out of your life of love, prolong my life.
Your words all add up to the sum total: Truth.
   Your righteous decisions are eternal.

+   +   +

161-168

I've been slandered unmercifully by the politicians,
   but my awe at your words keeps me stable.
I'm ecstatic over what you say,
   like one who strikes it rich.
I hate lies—can't stand them!—
   but I love what you have revealed.
Seven times each day I stop and shout praises
   for the way you keep everything running right.
For those who love what you reveal, everything fits—
   no stumbling around in the dark for them.
I wait expectantly for your salvation;
   GOD, I do what you tell me.
My soul guards and keeps all your instructions—
   oh, how much I love them!
I follow your directions, abide by your counsel;
   my life's an open book before you.

+   +   +

169-176

Let my cry come right into your presence, GOD;
   provide me with the insight that comes only from your Word.
Give my request your personal attention,
   rescue me on the terms of your promise.
Let praise cascade off my lips;
   after all, you've taught me the truth about life!
And let your promises ring from my tongue;
   every order you've given is right.
Put your hand out and steady me
   since I've chosen to live by your counsel.
I'm homesick, GOD, for your salvation;
   I love it when you show yourself!
Invigorate my soul so I can praise you well,
   use your decrees to put iron in my soul.
And should I wander off like a lost sheep—seek me!
   I'll recognize the sound of your voice.

A PILGRIM SONG

1-2

120
I'm in trouble. I cry to GOD,
   desperate for an answer:
"Deliver me from the liars, GOD!
   They smile so sweetly but lie through their teeth."

3-4

Do you know what's next, can you see what's coming,
   all you bold-faced liars?

Pointed arrows and burning coals
    will be your reward.

5-7 I'm doomed to live in Meshech,
    cursed with a home in Kedar,
My whole life lived camping
    among quarreling neighbors.
I'm all for peace, but the minute
    I tell them so, they go to war!

A PILGRIM SONG

1-2 **121** I look up to the mountains;
    does my strength come from mountains?
No, my strength comes from GOD,
    who made heaven, and earth, and mountains.

3-4 He won't let you stumble,
    your Guardian God won't fall asleep.
Not on your life! Israel's
    Guardian will never doze or sleep.

5-6 GOD's your Guardian,
    right at your side to protect you—
Shielding you from sunstroke,
    sheltering you from moonstroke.

7-8 GOD guards you from every evil,
    he guards your very life.
He guards you when you leave and when
    you return,
    he guards you now, he guards you always.

A PILGRIM SONG OF DAVID

1-2 **122** When they said, "Let's go to the house of GOD,"
    my heart leaped for joy.
And now we're here, O Jerusalem,
    inside Jerusalem's walls!

3-5 Jerusalem, well-built city,
    built as a place for worship!
The city to which the tribes ascend,
    all GOD's tribes go up to worship,
To give thanks to the name of GOD—
    this is what it means to be Israel.
Thrones for righteous judgment
    are set there, famous David-thrones.

6-9 Pray for Jerusalem's peace!
    Prosperity to all you Jerusalem-lovers!
Friendly insiders, get along!
    Hostile outsiders, keep your distance!

PILGRIM SONGS,

Pilgrimages happen in lots of different ways—some are physical journeys, some more spiritual or conceptual. They're more than merely "going somewhere," though, and the focus is often on what happens during the journey rather than the destination. A pilgrimage isn't a short trip; it's a long one that will likely have some challenges along the way. Many people of faith define their spiritual life as a journey or pilgrimage. There may be ups and downs, even portions of the journey that seem impossible to get through. But we know that our help comes from God and that God's help is available throughout the journey, even—maybe especially— in the hard parts.

PSALM 121

What do you notice about God in this psalm?

② Why do you think the writer starts out by asking where their strength comes from instead of just listing all the ways God helps?

PART ONE: JOURNEYS

③ What help could you ask God for on your own faith pilgrimage?

For the sake of my family and friends,
   I say it again: live in peace!
For the sake of the house of our God, GOD,
   I'll do my very best for you.

A PILGRIM SONG

123 I look to you, heaven-dwelling God,
   look up to you for help.
Like servants, alert to their master's commands,
   like a maiden attending her lady,
We're watching and waiting, holding
      our breath,
   awaiting your word of mercy.
Mercy, GOD, mercy!
   We've been kicked around long enough,
Kicked in the teeth by complacent rich men,
   kicked when we're down by arrogant brutes.

1-4

A PILGRIM SONG OF DAVID

124 If GOD hadn't been for us
      —all together now, Israel, sing out!—
If GOD hadn't been for us
   when everyone went against us,
We would have been swallowed alive
   by their violent anger,
Swept away by the flood of rage,
   drowned in the torrent;
We would have lost our lives
   in the wild, raging water.

1-5

6 Oh, blessed be GOD!
   He didn't go off and leave us.
He didn't abandon us defenseless,
   helpless as a rabbit in a pack of snarling dogs.

7 We've flown free from their fangs,
   free of their traps, free as a bird.
Their grip is broken;
   we're free as a bird in flight.

8 GOD's strong name is our help,
   the same GOD who made heaven and earth.

A PILGRIM SONG

125 Those who trust in GOD
      are like Zion Mountain:
Nothing can move it, a rock-solid mountain
   you can always depend on.
Mountains encircle Jerusalem,
   and GOD encircles his people—
   always has and always will.

1-5

The fist of the wicked
  will never violate
What is due the righteous,
  provoking wrongful violence.
Be good to your good people, GOD,
  to those whose hearts are right!
GOD will round up the backsliders,
  corral them with the incorrigibles.
Peace over Israel!

A PILGRIM SONG

126 It seemed like a dream, too good to be true,
  when GOD returned Zion's exiles. *(1-3)*
We laughed, we sang,
  we couldn't believe our good fortune.
We were the talk of the nations—
  "GOD was wonderful to them!"
GOD *was* wonderful to us;
  we are one happy people.

And now, GOD, do it again— *(4-6)*
  bring rains to our drought-stricken lives
So those who planted their crops in despair
  will shout "Yes!" at the harvest,
So those who went off with heavy hearts
  will come home laughing, with armloads of blessing.

A PILGRIM SONG OF SOLOMON

127 If GOD doesn't build the house,
  the builders only build shacks. *(1-2)*
If GOD doesn't guard the city,
  the night watchman might as well nap.
It's useless to rise early and go to bed late,
  and work your worried fingers to the bone.
Don't you know he enjoys
  giving rest to those he loves?

Don't you see that children are GOD's best gift? *(3-5)*
  the fruit of the womb his generous legacy?
Like a warrior's fistful of arrows
  are the children of a vigorous youth.
Oh, how blessed are you parents,
  with your quivers full of children!
Your enemies don't stand a chance against you;
  you'll sweep them right off your doorstep.

A PILGRIM SONG

128 All you who fear GOD, how blessed you are!
  how happily you walk on his smooth straight road! *(1-2)*
You worked hard and deserve all you've got coming.
  Enjoy the blessing! Soak in the goodness!

PILGRIM SONGS, PART TWO: REMINDERS

This psalm falls right in the middle of a collection of "road trip" songs that the ancient Israelites would sing on their journeys to Jerusalem for holidays and festivals. It's like your favorite playlist, except the little verses and choruses point to your family history and faith in God. This short but powerful song reminded the ancient singers—as it does us today—that God is the one who brings meaning to every moment of life. Without God, we're missing everything. We can imagine that as the Israelite people were walking, the reminders in this psalm kept them motivated to believe that their long journey to worship was truly worth it.

PSALM 127

3
How can you remind yourself of your need for God on a regular basis?

Why do you think it was important for the ancient Israelites to be reminded of their need for God?
1

2
What does it look like to depend on God in our modern world?

Your wife will bear children as a vine bears grapes,
  your household lush as a vineyard,
The children around your table
  as fresh and promising as young olive shoots.
Stand in awe of God's Yes.
  Oh, how he blesses the one who fears GOD!

3-4

Enjoy the good life in Jerusalem
  every day of your life.
And enjoy your grandchildren.
  Peace to Israel!

5-6

A PILGRIM SONG

129 "They've kicked me around ever since I was young"
    —this is how Israel tells it—
"They've kicked me around ever since I was young,
  but they never could keep me down.
Their plowmen plowed long furrows
  up and down my back;
But GOD wouldn't put up with it,
  he sticks with us.
Then GOD ripped the harnesses
  of the evil plowmen to shreds."

1-4

Oh, let all those who hate Zion
  grovel in humiliation;
Let them be like grass in shallow ground
  that withers before the harvest,
Before the farmhands can gather it in,
  the harvesters get in the crop,
Before the neighbors have a chance to call out,
  "Congratulations on your wonderful crop!
  We bless you in GOD's name!"

5-8

A PILGRIM SONG

130 Help, GOD—I've hit rock bottom!
    Master, hear my cry for help!
Listen hard! Open your ears!
  Listen to my cries for mercy.

1-2

If you, GOD, kept records on wrongdoings,
  who would stand a chance?
As it turns out, forgiveness is your habit,
  and that's why you're worshiped.

3-4

I pray to GOD—my life a prayer—
  and wait for what he'll say and do.
My life's on the line before God, my Lord,
  waiting and watching till morning,
  waiting and watching till morning.

5-6

PILGRIM SONGS, PART THREE: UNDERDOGS

We all love a good underdog story. They make for the best movies and books. They inspire us. They encourage us to never give up. This psalm did the same for the ancient Israelites. As they sang it, they'd be reminded of the fact that God took them from worst to first. They'd been through terrible lows in life, but God always seemed to find a way to restore them and bring them hope. Thankfully, God does the same for us today. When life gets tough, things may not get better right away, but we can be confident that God is still writing our stories.

PSALM 129

What effect do you think this psalm had on the Israelite people?

3 How does this psalm give you hope for whatever you're facing today?

2 Why do underdog stories tend to inspire us?

PILGRIM SONGS, PART FOUR: EARWORMS

Have you ever had a song stuck in your head? Some people call those "earworms," which, yes, sounds gross. Songs have a unique ability to allow us to both worship *and* remind ourselves of important qualities of God at the same time. That's what we see in many of the Psalms. Psalm 130 is a song focused on God's forgiveness and the hope that it brings. In singing this song, the Israelites were reminded that God forgives generously and were moved to worship. God's merciful forgiveness is an attribute we need to be reminded of regularly. Even though "earworms" sound icky, maybe we all need songs like this one stuck in our heads.

PSALM 130

What effect does remembering God's forgiveness have on this psalmist?

1

2

How does looking through the lens of what Jesus has accomplished deepen this psalm for us?

3

If this psalm became your song today, how might it help you experience the freedom God's forgiveness brings?

7-8 O Israel, wait and watch for GOD—
with GOD's arrival comes love,
with GOD's arrival comes generous
redemption.
No doubt about it—he'll redeem Israel,
buy back Israel from captivity to sin.

A PILGRIM SONG

1 **131** GOD, I'm not trying to rule the roost,
I don't want to be king of the mountain.
I haven't meddled where I have no business
or fantasized grandiose plans.

2 I've kept my feet on the ground,
I've cultivated a quiet heart.
Like a baby content in its mother's arms,
my soul is a baby content.

3 Wait, Israel, for GOD. Wait with hope.
Hope now; hope always!

A PILGRIM SONG

1-5 **132** O GOD, remember David,
remember all his troubles!
And remember how he promised GOD,
made a vow to the Strong God of Jacob,
"I'm not going home,
and I'm not going to bed,
I'm not going to sleep,
not even take time to rest,
Until I find a home for GOD,
a house for the Strong God of Jacob."

6-7 Remember how we got the news in Ephrathah,
learned all about it at Jaar Meadows?
We shouted, "Let's go to the shrine dedication!
Let's worship at God's own footstool!"

8-10 Up, GOD, enjoy your new place of quiet repose,
you and your mighty covenant ark;
Get your priests all dressed up in justice;
prompt your worshipers to sing this prayer:
"Honor your servant David;
don't disdain your anointed one."

11-18 GOD gave David his word,
he won't back out on this promise:
"One of your sons
I will set on your throne;
If your sons stay true to my Covenant
and learn to live the way I teach them,

PILGRIM SONGS, PART FIVE: GROUNDED

There are times when we need to dream big dreams and think big thoughts. There are times when we need to take control and make important things happen. There are times when we need to see ourselves as strong and powerful. But there are also times when it is important to keep our feet on the ground. There are times when we need to be realistic, times when we need to know and respect our limits. That's one of the messages of this psalm. Pay attention to where you are, and learn the difference between the time to dream and the time to be practical and realistic.

PSALM 131

Do you think this psalmist feels inspired, frustrated, or something else altogether?

③ When was a time you needed to dream big? When was a time you needed to be practical?

② If you were writing this psalm, what metaphors would you use?

Their sons will continue the line—
  always a son to sit on your throne.
Yes—I, GOD, chose Zion,
  the place I wanted for my shrine;
This will always be my home;
  this is what I want, and I'm here for good.
I'll shower blessings on the pilgrims who
    come here,
  and give supper to those who arrive hungry;
I'll dress my priests in salvation clothes;
  the holy people will sing their hearts out!
Oh, I'll make the place radiant for David!
  I'll fill it with light for my anointed!
I'll dress his enemies in dirty rags,
  but I'll make his crown sparkle with splendor."

A PILGRIM SONG OF DAVID

1-3 **133** How wonderful, how beautiful,
      when brothers and sisters get along!
It's like costly anointing oil
  flowing down head and beard,
Flowing down Aaron's beard,
  flowing down the collar of his priestly robes.
It's like the dew on Mount Hermon
  flowing down the slopes of Zion.
Yes, that's where GOD commands the blessing,
  ordains eternal life.

A PILGRIM SONG

1-3 **134** Come, bless GOD,
      all you servants of GOD!
You priests of GOD, posted to the nightwatch
  in GOD's shrine,
Lift your praising hands to the Holy Place,
  and bless GOD.
In turn, may GOD of Zion bless you—
  GOD who made heaven and earth!

1-4 **135** Hallelujah!
      Praise the name of GOD,
  praise the works of GOD.
All you priests on duty in GOD's temple,
  serving in the sacred halls of our God,
Shout "Hallelujah!" because GOD's so good,
  sing anthems to his beautiful name.
And why? Because GOD chose Jacob,
  embraced Israel as a prize possession.

5-12 I, too, give witness to the greatness of GOD,
      our Lord, high above all other gods.

He does just as he pleases—
    however, wherever, whenever.
He makes the weather—clouds and thunder,
    lightning and rain, wind pouring out of the north.
He struck down the Egyptian firstborn,
    both human and animal firstborn.
He made Egypt sit up and take notice,
    confronted Pharaoh and his servants
        with miracles.
Yes, he struck down great nations,
    he slew mighty kings—
Sihon king of the Amorites, also Og of Bashan—
    every last one of the Canaanite kings!
Then he turned their land over to Israel,
    a gift of good land to his people.

God, your name is eternal,   13-18
    God, you'll never be out-of-date.
God stands up for his people,
    God holds the hands of his people.
The gods of the godless nations are mere trinkets,
    made for quick sale in the markets:
Chiseled mouths that can't talk,
    painted eyes that can't see,
Carved ears that can't hear—
    dead wood! cold metal!
Those who make and trust them
    become like them.

Family of Israel, bless God!   19-21
    Family of Aaron, bless God!
Family of Levi, bless God!
    You who fear God, bless God!
Oh, blessed be God of Zion,
    First Citizen of Jerusalem!
Hallelujah!

136 Thank God! He deserves your thanks.   1-3
    His love never quits.
Thank the God of all gods,
    His love never quits.
Thank the Lord of all lords.
    His love never quits.

Thank the miracle-working God,   4-22
    His love never quits.
The God whose skill formed the cosmos,
    His love never quits.
The God who laid out earth on ocean foundations,
    His love never quits.

The God who filled the skies with light,
His love never quits.
The sun to watch over the day,
His love never quits.
Moon and stars as guardians of the night,
His love never quits.
The God who struck down the Egyptian firstborn,
His love never quits.
And rescued Israel from Egypt's oppression,
His love never quits.
Took Israel in hand with his powerful hand,
His love never quits.
Split the Red Sea right in half,
His love never quits.
Led Israel right through the middle,
His love never quits.
Dumped Pharaoh and his army in the sea,
His love never quits.
The God who marched his people through the desert,
His love never quits.
Smashed huge kingdoms right and left,
His love never quits.
Struck down the famous kings,
His love never quits.
Struck Sihon the Amorite king,
His love never quits.
Struck Og the Bashanite king,
His love never quits.
Then distributed their land as booty,
His love never quits.
Handed the land over to Israel.
His love never quits.

23-26 God remembered us when we were down,
His love never quits.
Rescued us from the trampling boot,
His love never quits.
Takes care of everyone in time of need.
His love never quits.
Thank God, who did it all!
His love never quits!

1-3 **137** Alongside Babylon's rivers
we sat on the banks; we cried and cried,
remembering the good old days in Zion.
Alongside the quaking aspens
we stacked our unplayed harps;
That's where our captors demanded songs,
sarcastic and mocking:
"Sing us a happy Zion song!"

Oh, how could we ever sing GOD's song 4-6
   in this wasteland?
If I ever forget you, Jerusalem,
   let my fingers wither and fall off like leaves.
Let my tongue swell and turn black
   if I fail to remember you,
If I fail, O dear Jerusalem,
   to honor you as my greatest.

GOD, remember those Edomites, 7-9
   and remember the ruin of Jerusalem,
That day they yelled out,
   "Wreck it, smash it to bits!"
And you, Babylonians—ravagers!
   A reward to whoever gets back at you
   for all you've done to us;
Yes, a reward to the one who grabs your babies
   and smashes their heads on the rocks!

A DAVID PSALM

138
Thank you! Everything in me says "Thank you!" 1-3
   Angels listen as I sing my thanks.
I kneel in worship facing your holy temple
   and say it again: "Thank you!"
Thank you for your love,
   thank you for your faithfulness;
Most holy is your name,
   most holy is your Word.
The moment I called out, you stepped in;
   you made my life large with strength.

When they hear what you have to say, GOD, 4-6
   all earth's kings will say "Thank you."
They'll sing of what you've done:
   "How great the glory of GOD!"
And here's why: GOD, high above, sees far below;
   no matter the distance, he knows everything about us.

When I walk into the thick of trouble, 7-8
   keep me alive in the angry turmoil.
With one hand
   strike my foes,
With your other hand
   save me.
Finish what you started in me, GOD.
   Your love is eternal—don't quit on me now.

A DAVID PSALM

139
GOD, investigate my life; 1-6
   get all the facts firsthand.
I'm an open book to you;

DON'T PRETEND

Why would people ask those in exile to sing a happy song?

PSALM 137

What do you notice about the tone of this psalm?

There are some things that happen in life that are just bad: moments when people harm us, cause us pain, or take away things we love. In times like those, there will always be someone who wants you to put on a happy face. Don't. There is nothing holy about pretending that bad things are good or that pain isn't significant. When you experience what the writer of this psalm is experiencing, don't sing a happy song. If you can sing, sing a song of mourning about the pain you've experienced. That pain is real and important; it shouldn't be ignored or pretended away.

Has there ever been a time in your life when you felt like you should pretend that a bad thing wasn't so bad?

even from a distance, you know what I'm thinking.
You know when I leave and when I get back;
   I'm never out of your sight.
You know everything I'm going to say
   before I start the first sentence.
I look behind me and you're there,
   then up ahead and you're there, too—
   your reassuring presence, coming and going.
This is too much, too wonderful—
   I can't take it all in!

Is there anyplace I can go to avoid your Spirit?   7-12
   to be out of your sight?
If I climb to the sky, you're there!
   If I go underground, you're there!
If I flew on morning's wings
   to the far western horizon,
You'd find me in a minute—
   you're already there waiting!
Then I said to myself, "Oh, he even sees me in the dark!
   At night I'm immersed in the light!"
It's a fact: darkness isn't dark to you;
   night and day, darkness and light, they're all the same
      to you.

Oh yes, you shaped me first inside, then out;   13-16
   you formed me in my mother's womb.
I thank you, High God—you're breathtaking!
   Body and soul, I am marvelously made!
   I worship in adoration—what a creation!
You know me inside and out,
   you know every bone in my body;
You know exactly how I was made, bit by bit,
   how I was sculpted from nothing into something.
Like an open book, you watched me grow from conception to birth;
   all the stages of my life were spread out before you,
The days of my life all prepared
   before I'd even lived one day.

Your thoughts—how rare, how beautiful!   17-22
   God, I'll never comprehend them!
I couldn't even begin to count them—
   any more than I could count the sand of the sea.
Oh, let me rise in the morning and live always with you!
   And please, God, do away with wickedness for good!
And you murderers—out of here!—
   all the men and women who belittle you, God,
   infatuated with cheap god-imitations.
See how I hate those who hate you, GOD,
   see how I loathe all this godless arrogance;

As you grow up, it's easy to feel like no one truly understands you. You might feel alone or like you're living in the shadows. Psalm 139 reminds us that God knows us *personally*. God knows our thoughts, knows where we go and what we do. God is always with us, in the light and in the dark. In fact, this psalmist says that even darkness isn't dark to God and that we're "immersed in the light" (Psalm 139:11). No matter what we're going through or how dark it feels, we're never alone. God's presence is always shining on us and guiding us home.

3
What's one way you can apply the message of Psalm 139 in your daily life?

2
What does it mean that even "darkness isn't dark" to God (Psalm 139:12)?

PSALM 139

1 How can the reminder that God knows you personally and is always with you bring comfort in times when you feel alone or misunderstood?

IMMERSED IN THE LIGHT

I hate it with pure, unadulterated hatred.
  Your enemies are my enemies!

Investigate my life, O God,   23-24
  find out everything about me;
Cross-examine and test me,
  get a clear picture of what I'm about;
See for yourself whether I've done anything wrong—
  then guide me on the road to eternal life.

A DAVID PSALM

140 GOD, get me out of here, away from this evil;   1-5
      protect me from these vicious people.
All they do is think up new ways to be bad;
  they spend their days plotting war games.
They practice the sharp rhetoric of hate and hurt,
  speak venomous words that maim and kill.
GOD, keep me out of the clutch of these wicked ones,
  protect me from these vicious people;
All boast and swagger, they plot ways to trip me up,
  determined to bring me down.
These crooks invent traps to catch me
  and do their best to incriminate me.

I prayed, "GOD, you're my God!   6-8
  Listen, GOD! Mercy!
GOD, my Lord, Strong Savior,
  protect me when the fighting breaks out!
Don't let the wicked have their way, GOD,
  don't give them an inch!"

These troublemakers all around me—   9-11
  let them drown in their own verbal poison.
Let God pile hellfire on them,
  let him bury them alive in crevasses!
These loudmouths—
  don't let them be taken seriously;
These savages—
  let the Devil hunt them down!

I know that you, GOD, are on the side of victims,   12-13
  that you care for the rights of the poor.
And I know that the righteous personally
    thank you,
  that good people are secure in your presence.

A DAVID PSALM

141 GOD, come close. Come quickly!   1-2
      Open your ears—it's my voice you're hearing!
Treat my prayer as sweet incense rising;
  my raised hands are my evening prayers.

3-7 Post a guard at my mouth, GOD,
    set a watch at the door of my lips.
Don't let me so much as dream of evil
    or thoughtlessly fall into bad company.
And these people who only do wrong—
    don't let them lure me with their sweet talk!
May the Just One set me straight,
    may the Kind One correct me,
Don't let sin anoint my head.
    I'm praying hard against their evil ways!
Oh, let their leaders be pushed off a high
      rock cliff;
    make them face the music.
Like a rock pulverized by a maul,
    let their bones be scattered at the gates
      of hell.

8-10 But GOD, dear Lord,
    I only have eyes for you.
Since I've run for dear life to you,
    take good care of me.
Protect me from their evil scheming,
    from all their demonic subterfuge.
Let the wicked fall flat on their faces,
    while I walk off without a scratch.

A DAVID PRAYER—WHEN HE WAS IN THE CAVE

1-2 **142** I cry out loudly to GOD,
    loudly I plead with GOD for mercy.
I spill out all my complaints before him,
    and spell out my troubles in detail:

3-7 "As I sink in despair, my spirit ebbing away,
    you know how I'm feeling,
Know the danger I'm in,
    the traps hidden in my path.
Look right, look left—
    there's not a soul who cares what happens!
I'm up against the wall, with no exit—
    it's just me, all alone.
I cry out, GOD, call out:
    'You're my last chance, my only hope for life!'
Oh listen, please listen;
    I've never been this low.
Rescue me from those who are hunting me down;
    I'm no match for them.
Get me out of this dungeon
    so I can thank you in public.
Your people will form a circle around me
    and you'll bring me showers of blessing!"

A DAVID PSALM

143

Listen to this prayer of mine, GOD;
   pay attention to what I'm asking.
Answer me—you're famous for your answers!
   Do what's right for me.
But don't, please don't, haul me into court;
   not a person alive would be acquitted there.

1-2

The enemy hunted me down;
   he kicked me and stomped me within an inch of my life.
He put me in a black hole,
   buried me like a corpse in that dungeon.
I sat there in despair, my spirit draining away,
   my heart heavy, like lead.
I remembered the old days,
   went over all you've done, pondered the ways
      you've worked,
Stretched out my hands to you,
   as thirsty for you as a desert thirsty for rain.

3-6

Hurry with your answer, GOD!
   I'm nearly at the end of my rope.
Don't turn away; don't ignore me!
   That would be certain death.
If you wake me each morning with the sound of your
      loving voice,
   I'll go to sleep each night trusting in you.
Point out the road I must travel;
   I'm all ears, all eyes before you.
Save me from my enemies, GOD—
   you're my only hope!
Teach me how to live to please you,
   because you're my God.
Lead me by your blessed Spirit
   into cleared and level pastureland.

7-10

Keep up your reputation, God—give me life!
   In your justice, get me out of this trouble!
In your great love, vanquish my enemies;
   make a clean sweep of those who harass me.
And why? Because I'm your servant.

11-12

A DAVID PSALM

144

Blessed be GOD, my mountain,
   who trains me to fight fair and well.
He's the bedrock on which I stand,
   the castle in which I live,
   my rescuing knight,
The high crag where I run for dear life,
   while he lays my enemies low.

1-2

3-4 I wonder why you care, GOD—
    why do you bother with us at all?
  All we are is a puff of air;
    we're like shadows in a campfire.

5-8 Step down out of heaven, GOD;
    ignite volcanoes in the hearts of the mountains.
  Hurl your lightnings in every direction;
    shoot your arrows this way and that.
  Reach all the way from sky to sea:
    pull me out of the ocean of hate,
    out of the grip of those barbarians
  Who lie through their teeth,
    who shake your hand
    then knife you in the back.

9-10 O God, let me sing a new song to you,
    let me play it on a twelve-string guitar—
  A song to the God who saved the king,
    the God who rescued David, his servant.

11 Rescue me from the enemy sword,
    release me from the grip of those barbarians
  Who lie through their teeth,
    who shake your hand
    then knife you in the back.

12-14 Make our sons in their prime
    like sturdy oak trees,
  Our daughters as shapely and bright
    as fields of wildflowers.
  Fill our barns with great harvest,
    fill our fields with huge flocks;
  Protect us from invasion and exile—
    eliminate the crime in our streets.

15 How blessed the people who have all this!
  How blessed the people who have GOD for God!

DAVID'S PRAISE

1 **145** I lift you high in praise, my God, O my King!
    and I'll bless your name into eternity.

2 I'll bless you every day,
    and keep it up from now to eternity.

3 GOD is magnificent; he can never be praised enough.
    There are no boundaries to his greatness.

4 Generation after generation stands in awe of your work;
    each one tells stories of your mighty acts.

Your beauty and splendor have everyone talking; 5
    I compose songs on your wonders.

Your marvelous doings are headline news; 6
    I could write a book full of the details of your greatness.

The fame of your goodness spreads across the country; 7
    your righteousness is on everyone's lips.

GOD is all mercy and grace— 8
    not quick to anger, is rich in love.

GOD is good to one and all; 9
    everything he does is soaked through
        with grace.

Creation and creatures applaud you, GOD; 10-11
    your holy people bless you.

They talk about the glories of your rule,
    they exclaim over your splendor,

Letting the world know of your power for good, 12
    the lavish splendor of your kingdom.

Your kingdom is a kingdom eternal; 13
    you never get voted out of office.

GOD always does what he says,
    and is gracious in everything he does.

GOD gives a hand to those down on their luck, 14
    gives a fresh start to those ready to quit.

All eyes are on you, expectant; 15
    you give them their meals on time.

Generous to a fault, 16
    you lavish your favor on all creatures.

Everything GOD does is right— 17
    the trademark on all his works is love.

GOD's there, listening for all who pray, 18
    for all who pray and mean it.

He does what's best for those who fear him— 19
    hears them call out, and saves them.

GOD sticks by all who love him, 20
    but it's all over for those who don't.

21   My mouth is filled with GOD's praise.
       Let everything living bless him,
         bless his holy name from now to eternity!

1-2 **146** Hallelujah!
               O my soul, praise GOD!
     All my life long I'll praise GOD,
       singing songs to my God as long as I live.

3-9 Don't put your life in the hands of experts
       who know nothing of life, of *salvation* life.
     Mere humans don't have what it takes;
       when they die, their projects die with them.
     Instead, get help from the God of Jacob,
       put your hope in GOD and know real blessing!
     GOD made sky and soil,
       sea and all the fish in it.
     He always does what he says—
       he defends the wronged,
       he feeds the hungry.
     GOD frees prisoners—
       he gives sight to the blind,
       he lifts up the fallen.
     GOD loves good people, protects strangers,
       takes the side of orphans and widows,
       but makes short work of the wicked.

10   GOD's in charge—*always.*
       Zion's God is God for good!
       Hallelujah!

1   **147** Hallelujah!
               It's a good thing to sing praise to our God;
       praise is beautiful, praise is fitting.

2-6 GOD's the one who rebuilds Jerusalem,
       who regathers Israel's scattered exiles.
     He heals the heartbroken
       and bandages their wounds.
     He counts the stars
       and assigns each a name.
     Our Lord is great, with limitless strength;
       we'll never comprehend what he knows
         and does.
     GOD puts the fallen on their feet again
       and pushes the wicked into the ditch.

7-11 Sing to GOD a thanksgiving hymn,
       play music on your instruments to God,
     Who fills the sky with clouds,
       preparing rain for the earth,

Then turning the mountains green with grass,
    feeding both cattle and crows.
He's not impressed with horsepower;
    the size of our muscles means little to him.
Those who fear GOD get GOD's attention;
    they can depend on his strength.

Jerusalem, worship GOD!   12-18
    Zion, praise your God!
He made your city secure,
    he blessed your children among you.
He keeps the peace at your borders,
    he puts the best bread on your tables.
He launches his promises earthward—
    how swift and sure they come!
He spreads snow like a white fleece,
    he scatters frost like ashes,
He broadcasts hail like birdseed—
    who can survive his winter?
Then he gives the command and it all melts;
    he breathes on winter—suddenly it's spring!

He speaks the same way to Jacob,   19-20
    speaks words that work to Israel.
He never did this to the other nations;
    they never heard such commands.
Hallelujah!

148 Hallelujah!   1-5
Praise GOD from heaven,
    praise him from the mountaintops;
Praise him, all you his angels,
    praise him, all you his warriors,
Praise him, sun and moon,
    praise him, you morning stars;
Praise him, high heaven,
    praise him, heavenly rain clouds;
Praise, oh let them praise the name of GOD—
    he spoke the word, and there they were!

He set them in place   6
    from all time to eternity;
He gave his orders,
    and that's it!

Praise GOD from earth,   7-12
    you sea dragons, you fathomless ocean deeps;
Fire and hail, snow and ice,
    hurricanes obeying his orders;
Mountains and all hills,
    apple orchards and cedar forests;

HALLELUJAH

PSALMS 146–150

Why do you think the Hallelujah Psalms come at the end of the book of Psalms?

2

3

When you think about what God has done, is doing, and will do in your life, what can you say hallelujah for?

The word *hallelujah* is the ultimate praise to God. It's a Hebrew expression that means "praise the Lord." It's mostly found in the book of Psalms. Psalms 146–150 are often called "Hallelujah Psalms" because they're filled with examples of what God has done for God's people in every aspect of their lives and express how, in return, God's people respond with thanksgiving, joy, and adoration. Saying hallelujah doesn't have to wait until Sunday worship. We can praise God every day for what God has done, what God is doing, and even for what God will do. Hallelujah!

1 What do you notice about the next few lines that follow the *hallelujah* at the beginning of each psalm?

Wild beasts and herds of cattle,
  snakes, and birds in flight;
Earth's kings and all races,
  leaders and important people,
Robust men and women in their prime,
  and yes, graybeards and little children.

Let them praise the name of GOD—   13-14
  it's the only Name worth praising.
His radiance exceeds anything in earth and sky;
  he's built a monument—his very own people!

Praise from all who love GOD!
  Israel's children, intimate friends of GOD.
Hallelujah!

149
Hallelujah!   1-4
  Sing to GOD a brand-new song,
praise him in the company of all who love him.
Let all Israel celebrate their Sovereign Creator,
  Zion's children exult in their King.
Let them praise his name in dance;
  strike up the band and make great music!
And why? Because GOD delights in his people,
  adorns plain folk with salvation garlands!

Let true lovers break out in praise,   5-9
  sing out from wherever they're sitting,
Shout the high praises of God,
  brandish their swords in the wild sword-dance—
A portent of vengeance on the God-defying nations,
  a signal that punishment's coming,
Their kings chained and hauled off to jail,
  their leaders behind bars for good,
The judgment on them carried out to the letter
  —and all who love God in the seat of honor!
Hallelujah!

150
Hallelujah!   1-6
  Praise God in his holy house of worship,
praise him under the open skies;
Praise him for his acts of power,
  praise him for his magnificent greatness;
Praise with a blast on the trumpet,
  praise by strumming soft strings;
Praise him with castanets and dance,
  praise him with banjo and flute;
Praise him with cymbals and a big bass drum,
  praise him with fiddles and mandolin.
Let every living, breathing creature praise GOD!
  Hallelujah!

THE MESSAGE STUDENT DEVOTIONAL BIBLE TEAM

OLIVIA ELDREDGE
Message Bible Editor

MARK OESTREICHER
Project Editor

DEAN H. RENNINGER
Art Director & Interior Designer

EVA M. WINTERS
Cover Designer

SARAH K. JOHNSON
Copyediting Coordinator

CATHY MILLER
Typesetter

JONATHAN BRYANT
Bible Editorial Consultant

LEANNE F. ROLLAND
DIANA E. JOHNSON
CAROLE NEWING JOHNSON
Copyeditors

VICTORIA MARTIN
Product Manager

CONTRIBUTOR BIOGRAPHIES

OLIVIA ELDREDGE is the managing editor for NavPress and oversees *Message* Bible product development at NavPress.

MARK OESTREICHER (Marko) is a veteran youth worker and founding partner of The Youth Cartel, providing coaching for church youth workers. The author of more than seventy books, Marko is a sought-after speaker, writer, and consultant. Marko lives in San Diego.

+ + +

ASHLEY BOHINC is a sought-after communicator, author, coach, and consultant with over twenty years of experience serving teenagers in educational, athletic, and ministry settings.

JEN BRADBURY is a pastor with over twenty years of experience in youth and family ministry. She's also the author or coauthor of several books, including *Faith beyond Youth Group*.

SARAH HAUGE is the former managing editor of The Youth Cartel and volunteered as a youth leader for more than ten years. She lives in Spokane, Washington.

MIKE E. HAYNES II is a youth ministry veteran, a published author, and the creator of G Shades Youth Ministry Curriculum.

CRYSTAL KIRGISS has a PhD from Purdue University and is the director of discipleship content for Young Life. She's a writer, teacher, and speaker for both teens and adults.

AQUEELAH LIGONDE is a professional coach, consultant, and speaker who partners with and empowers leaders and congregations as they live into their fullest God-given potential.

KATIE MATSUMOTO MOORE is a pastor with fifteen years of ministry experience. She and her husband, Kellen, serve the next generation in Southern California.

SHANE SANCHEZ, an author with over fifteen years of experience in student ministry, is passionate about helping students find thriving life in Jesus. He balances his roles as a speaker and thought leader in global youth ministry with those of being a dedicated husband and father.

MARTIN SAUNDERS is an author, a speaker, and the founding director of Satellites, a British event that helps young people live Jesus-centered lives.

JOHN SORRELL led youth ministry for twenty years and has a PhD in New Testament interpretation. He enjoys encouraging students and families to pursue the full life that Jesus talks about.

JEREMY STEELE has, for over twenty-five years, helped parents, individuals, and organizations communicate with younger generations about God and life. He is the church and culture translator for The Changemaker Initiative.

INDEX OF DEVOTIONAL ENTRIES

THE TRANSLATOR AND HIS FRIENDS

EUGENE H. PETERSON was a pastor, scholar, writer, and poet. After teaching at a seminary and then giving nearly thirty years to church ministry in the Baltimore area, he created *The Message: The Bible in Contemporary Language*—a vibrant Bible translation that connects with today's readers like no other. It took Eugene a full ten years to complete. He worked from the Greek and Hebrew texts to ensure authenticity. At the same time, his ear was always tuned to the cadence and energy of contemporary English.

Eugene wrote more than thirty books, including *As Kingfishers Catch Fire*, *Run with the Horses*, and *A Long Obedience in the Same Direction*. For his work on *The Message*, he received the prestigious ECPA Gold Medallion Book Award.

Eugene served as Professor of Spiritual Theology at Regent College in Vancouver, BC, retiring in 2006. He spent his final years in Montana with his beloved wife, Jan.

TRANSLATION CONSULTANTS
Peterson's work has been thoroughly reviewed by the following team of recognized Old and New Testament scholars, who ensured that it is accurate as well as faithful to the original languages.

OLD TESTAMENT TEAM
Robert L. Hubbard Jr., *North Park Theological Seminary* (chair)
Richard E. Averbeck, *Trinity Evangelical Divinity School*
Bryan E. Beyer, *Columbia International University*
Lamar E. Cooper Sr., *Criswell College*
Peter E. Enns, *Eastern University*
Duane E. Garrett, *The Southern Baptist Theological Seminary*
Donald R. Glenn, *Dallas Theological Seminary*
Paul R. House, *Beeson Divinity School, Samford University*
V. Phillips Long, *Regent College*
Tremper Longman III, *Westmont College*
John N. Oswalt, *Asbury Theological Seminary*
Richard L. Pratt Jr., *Reformed Theological Seminary*
John H. Walton, *Wheaton College*
Prescott H. Williams Jr., *Austin Presbyterian Theological Seminary*
Marvin R. Wilson, *Gordon College*

NEW TESTAMENT TEAM
William W. Klein, *Denver Seminary* (chair)
Darrell L. Bock, *Dallas Theological Seminary*
Donald A. Hagner, *Fuller Theological Seminary*
Moisés Silva, *Gordon-Conwell Theological Seminary*
Rodney A. Whitacre, *Trinity School for Ministry*

Continue Reading
The Message Student Devotional Bible

The Message combines the authority of God's Word with the cadence and energy of conversational English. Experience the full Bible with all the *Message Student Devotional* content!

New supplemental features make this a highly usable and engaging resource for students. A carefully selected network of youth ministry professionals deliver devotional content with a beautiful and contemporary design.

Key Features
- introductions to every book of the Bible
- 320 devotions with guided reflection on key Bible passages
- Eugene Peterson's introduction to *The Message* and a supplemental essay on the Bible's relevance for today's students
- 30 character profiles that can serve as a 30-day devotional
- the full text of *The Message* in a highly readable typesetting

CP2001